The Art
of
Product
Management

Lessons from a
Silicon Valley Innovator

Rich Mironov

Enthiosys Press
Mountain View, California

ISBN 1-4392-1606-1

*To Marcia, source of all good things,
and Sasha, my Chief Analogy Officer*

Table of Contents

Introduction by Henry Chesbrough VI

Foreword by David Strom X

Preface XII

SECTION ONE: Falling in Love 2

    Parenting and the Art of Product Management..................... 5

    Early Selling: Thoroughbreds and Explorers 11

    Burning Your Boats 17

    Avoiding the Post-Course Correction 23

    Why are there Serial Entrepreneurs?.................................. 29

    Owning the Gap 35

    Girls Getting a Head Start (-Up) 41

SECTION TWO: Organizing your Organization 44

    Where Should PM Report?.. 47

    The Roadmap Less Traveled 55

    Crowding Out Tech Support 61

    Product Management is Inherently Political 69

    Defensive Processes 77

    Growing Back into Management 85

    Who's Calling Customer Support?..................................... 91

    Hallucinogenic Funding 97

SECTION THREE: The Almost-New-New Things.................... 102

    The Accidental Agilist... 105

    A Planetary View of Agile Product Management 113

    Burning Through Product Managers 119

    Grocers and Chefs: Software Service Models..................... 125

    So Your Product Wants to Be a Service............................. 131

    The "Null Service" 137

SECTION FOUR: Getting into Customers' Heads.................. 142

    Getting into Customers' Heads... 145

    Sharks, Pilot Fish and the Product Food Chain 149

    Insider Thinking 157

The Strategic Secret Shopper 163
Avoiding a Ticking B-O-M 169
Technical Advantage and Competitive Strategy........................... 173
Mo' Beta 179
SECTION FIVE: What Should Things Cost?........................... 184
"Goldilocks" Packaging 187
What's Your Pricing Metric? 193
Risk-Sharing and Customer-Perceived Value................................. 199
Sales-Friendly Price Lists.. 205
Afterword 211
Acknowledgements... 213
About the Author 215

Introduction

HENRY CHESBROUGH

Adjunct Professor and Executive Director,
Center for Open Innovation, Haas School of Business, UC Berkeley

There are lots of books (some of them quite good) on the importance of innovation for business success. I myself have written a few. Indeed, it's hard to find anyone who has a bad word to say about innovation these days. As we head into choppy economic waters, though, it is not enough to know that innovation is important. We also need to understand what specifically needs to be done, and how best to get that done.

One area where innovation gets down to business, is in the arena of "product management". This amorphous term is the label applied to some of the most important work that goes on in the innovation process when developing and introducing a new product (or, for that matter, managing an existing product). The product management function is responsible for uncovering and articulating the market's need for a new product or service. At the same time, product managers work closely with engineering to discern the technical possibilities and challenges facing the new product. The product manager must dance between the technical organization inside, and the world of the customer outside. Done poorly, product management can waste time and money, and deliver a product that few people wish to buy. Done well, product management leads to products that people want, that work well in their intended use, and become profitable businesses for the company.

This is where my friend and colleague of long standing, Rich Mironov, comes in. Like me, he agrees that innovation is important. Like me, he has "been there", working in the trenches in a variety of product management functions across a range of Silicon Valley companies. His career spans nearly a quarter century (I barely lasted a decade before moving into academia). Rich's experience and success have made him a thought leader among technology practitioners. While he has extensive experience, he also possesses a unique ability to reflect upon that experience to uncover more systematic insights into the sources of success and failure in developing products and launching startup companies. And while he is highly skilled in understanding technology, his deepest insights relate to the human heart - and how people (and their motivations) affect technology products and vice versa. I currently teach at the Haas School of Business at UC Berkeley, and Rich has been a frequent guest lecturer in both the MBA and the executive education classrooms there.

When you read this book, you'll see the wisdom he has accumulated along with his considerable scar tissue. I promise you that there is nothing else out there quite like it.

I remember reading the first installment of what was then called Product Bytes, back in 2002. I became an immediate and enthusiastic fan. These pieces are short, to the point, with a light touch, that nonetheless lead to very important and actionable insights. Most of these insights were learned the hard way by Rich. But throughout this book, you'll see that he never becomes cynical or disillusioned. Like me, he believes in his heart that we must innovate to continue to advance, though there will be plenty of roadblocks and snafus along the way. With this book, Rich shares with you some of the lessons he has learned. Anyone wrestling with developing new products, or launching a new startup company, will find this an invaluable resource to return to again and again. I predict you'll laugh, perhaps cry, and emerge a little wiser each time you read from this book.

Foreword

DAVID STROM

There are a lot of computer-related books on the market. But there are very few of them that actually teach you how to market software and hardware products and not repeat the mistakes of the past.

I've known Rich through several jobs over the past ten years, and now can be outed as his unofficial writing coach. I told him before he started his monthly newsletter, Product Bytes, that he needed to make sure that this was something he wanted to do. I suggested he write the first three issues, and if he still had something to say, then he was probably going to succeed at the effort. Ten years later, he is still going strong.

Good writing is often overlooked by product people, even though it can help you define your ultimate customer base, understand your product's feature set, and explain why you need certain resources to tell your story and differentiate your products. Maybe I am more sensitive to bad writing than others – after all, I didn't start out my career as a writer. Au contraire, I was a math and engineering major in college and it wasn't until my mid-20s that I learned how to write. It was a hard-acquired skill, and one that requires daily practice if you are going to be good, let alone great, at it. I am lucky that I am able to make a living at my writing, and that there are still plenty of interesting products to test and write about after being in the IT industry for more than 25 years.

Anyway, enough about me. This book is well worth your time. It is chock full of practical advice, and should be a bible for computer product managers, even those that are already parents of small children and think they are good at that unpaid job.

Part of Rich's message is that the product is really secondary to the people who work at the company. One of the reasons why Dilbert still continues to resonate with high-tech workers is that there are so many bad managers, or managers who don't understand how to mentor and develop their staff.

The whirl of Web 2.0 and social networks have made this problem worse, rather than better. LinkedIn and Facebook have made it easier to move to another job and stay in touch with your former colleagues – I just heard from someone that I worked with 25 years and countless number of job changes ago. Email has become second nature. It is easier to surround ourselves with screens rather than get out of our cubicles and have some face time with a co-worker.

If we have learned anything from the dot-bomb bust years at the beginning of this decade, it is that companies need to pay more attention to the marketing of their products. We are no longer in an era of "build-it-and-they-will-download". Take some time to review Rich's precepts, and see if you can do a better job of parenting your products. ❧

David is an international authority on network and Internet technologies. He has written extensively on the topic for 20 years for a wide variety of print publications and websites, such as The New York Times, TechTarget.com, PC Week/eWeek, Internet.com, Network World, Infoworld, Computerworld, Small Business Computing, Communications Week, Windows Sources, c | net and news.com, Web Review, Tom's Hardware, EETimes, and many others. He is the author of two books: Internet Messaging (Prentice Hall, 1998) which he co-authored with Marshall T. Rose and Home Networking Survival Guide (McGrawHill/Osborne, 2001).

Preface

I'm a repeat offender at technology start-ups. That includes being "the product guy" at four very early stage companies, and consulting to product and technical teams at more than two dozen other companies.

A MOMENT IN TIME

In September 2001, I left a VP Marketing/Product Management job at my third start-up. This was a very difficult time: throughout Silicon Valley, you could hear the whoosh of the first Internet Bubble deflating. All that year, high-concept start-ups were being padlocked faster than movers could haul away Aeron chairs. The Twin Towers had just come down, and irrational exuberance was in very short supply. I was an unattached product guy, and didn't see any intriguing start-ups worthy of an emotional commitment. Suddenly, I was a product management consultant.

After two decades in Silicon Valley technical and product roles, I was able to tap my personal network for lots of interesting projects. It was immediately clear, though, that very **few people knew what technology product managers really do**, and why they are critical to Silicon Valley's success. Even savvy entrepreneurs and Engineering VPs had trouble recognizing the symptoms of inadequate product management. Shockingly, most of my product management peers were also unable to explain their value clearly enough to get the respect they deserved.

In dozens of breakfasts and lunches, I tried and failed to describe the essence of product managers: the honest brokers who balance customer needs with engineering realities, market requirements with financial goals. We were the handful of matrixed product champions and driver-drivers who push great things out the door. Truth-tellers in the executive suite. It became clear to me that the product management story is best told as a series of vignettes.

Out of this swirl, Product Bytes was born. My goal was to find a thousand words each month that captured one small part of the product management challenge. And it caught on. Product managers added themselves to the distribution list[1] because they recognized themselves in these monthly stories. Engineering and management folks signed up to learn a little more about the strange animals they work with.

---

1. This was before RSS had been widely adopted.

This book compiles some of my most popular columns from 2002 to 2008. It includes thoughts on building and maintaining product organizations, understanding how customers think, ideas for how to price new products, and ways to motivate people who don't work for you. (Typically, no one works for a product manager.) Collected into a single volume, it paints a picture of a typical interrupt-driven day.

So what is a product manager? As you'll see, that's a difficult question to answer briefly. My closest analogy is to parenting: the product manager is responsible for the long-term development and health of a product, and is constantly faced with co-workers (or customers or partners or company executives) who want short cuts to good results. Every parent knows that kids need time to grow and develop – and rushing them doesn't usually help. I've recapped "*Parenting and the Art of Product Management*" thousands of times, and still believe that "**we're not really parents [or product managers] until we've gotten some poop on our hands and laughed about it.**"

Likewise, start-ups are radically different than established companies in ways that can be difficult to describe to non-participants. Folks at tiny companies are more invested in the day-to-day survival of their organizations (and not just in terms of pre-IPO stock). One of my earliest pieces on this difference was "*Thoroughbreds and Explorers*", which highlights the hungry and creative generalists that start-ups need. Over the years, I've returned to start-ups many times – both as the first "product guy" and as a consultant – for a hit of that pure entrepreneurial spirit.

Pushing that analogy a bit further, I'm deeply appreciative of the pioneering spirit of entrepreneurs and technologists worldwide. Software development's unofficial headquarters is still here in Silicon Valley, but with branch offices in Bangalore and Ramat Gan and Shanghai and Prague and Kiev and many other places. I'm lucky to be part of a far-flung but tightly networked community of product managers who speak the same language, and share a love of great solutions.

By the way, during 2008 we've finally seen some important software development trends going mainstream, especially Agile and Software-as-a-Service. There are some early discussions of these throughout the book, in their original pre-buzz-word form. Since Product Bytes is an ongoing conversation, you'll be reading more from me about Agile in 2009, so I hope that you'll join the discussion at www.ProductBytes.com and www.Enthiosys.com.

So. Enough about my last release. Let me tell you about my next release...

Rich Mironov

Falling in Love
Start-Ups and Product Management

SECTION ONE

Joining a start-up is like falling in love. Product managers at start-ups need to be passionate about their products/services, spending every minute of their days cajoling their teams to create wonderful products [inward-looking] or telling the world how wonderful those products will be [outward-looking]. This is hard, repetitive, and often thankless. For me, it's never been as simple as work-for-pay. Product managers who don't love their products should change product lines or companies - or careers.

On the departure side, leaving a startup is like ending a serious romance. Whether you leave voluntarily or not, you may find yourself emotionally bruised and not quite ready to love again. More determined to be a little choosier when picking your next start-up. Each time I've walked out the door, I've tried to take some time to consult, write, teach, and mourn just a tiny bit. That's eventually followed by dozens of meetings with entrepreneurs at new companies ("speed dating") and the occasional interim executive role ("going steady").

In any case, product managers are an odd mix of enthusiasm and persistence, unfounded hope and grim financial realities. Their emotional cycles start to line up with product release plans. Sane people look at this role and shake their heads in disbelief. I hope that you recognize yourself in the following pages.

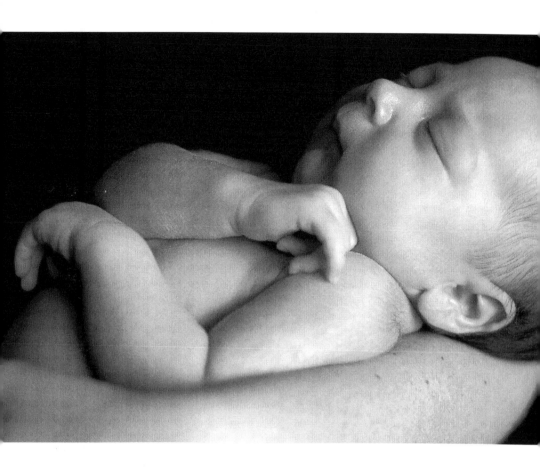

Parenting and the Art of Product Management

AUGUST 2003

Over the years, I've told variations of this story many times: being a product manager is a lot like being a parent. We love our products, make multi-year commitments to their development, hide their shortcomings, and look out for their best long-term interests while other organizations live in the moment. We groom our products for good mergers later in life — and may be heartbroken by market indifference or eventual end-of-life.

Not everyone wants to raise children or enterprise software. Consider the following observations before volunteering for high-tech parenthood…

BOOK LEARNING IS NO SUBSTITUTE FOR EXPERIENCE

Parents-to-be are often deluged with "how to" books offering sage advice. These offer helpful vignettes about feeding, sleeping, discipline, and how to get strained peas out of your hair. The reality of children is impossible to distill into a book, though. Stated more colorfully, **we're not really parents until we've gotten some poop on our hands and laughed about it**.

Likewise there are lots of articles about pricing strategy, positioning, market segmentation, and how to prioritize an endless feature request list. (*Present company included.*) When the time comes, though, your situation is always unique. You'll eventually have to recommend a pricing model and defend it, so get started. Be humble, but don't apologize for a less-than-perfect first effort.

If you're lucky enough to find a mentor, ask for the war stories. *"What didn't work and why? How is this product like yours? What templates can I borrow?"* Except in the largest companies that maintain very strong processes, book learning is over-rated.

ALLOWING TIME TO CRAWL, THEN WALK

Most babies can't sing or pole vault or read Sanskrit. And we don't expect them to. We encourage their first steps, applaud "chopsticks," sign them up for fingerpainting or swimming lessons. We try to uncover their secret talents. We know that they will make lots of mistakes. In fact, we've signed up for decades of bruised knees, failed science projects, dreadful school plays and disastrous first dates.

Technical products also grow up. It's a rare for anything to be complete in its first release, and even rarer for you to anticipate the right audience for your new baby. The first year (or two) are spent bumping into markets, fixing bugs, talking with customers, and discovering unexpected niches for your brainchild.

(Microsoft has certainly taught us not to expect any product to be usable before version 3.1.)

Part of your responsibility as a PM is to protect and nurture your baby. Set appropriate expectations for beta customers. Have a developmental roadmap that shows when more features will arrive. Try to read product reviews calmly. Don't throw the software out with the bug report. If you're not proud of your wunder-kind, then no one will be.

IN IT FOR THE LONG TERM

As parents, we're committed to deferred gratification and multi-year planning. We show our faith in the future by moving into good school districts, saving for college, and insisting that geometry is worth learning. Part of our job is to make some long-term plans and thoughtfully trade off the present for the future. Children want immediate gratification, so we have to make some choices for them.

As a product manager, you're in similar territory. Faced with an infinitely long list of feature requests, you must help developers stick to the important items and minimize "feature creep." Sketching out the next half-dozen releases can comfort pouting customers who want everything right away.

A good friend with a 7-year-old reminded me that preparing dinner once for your child can be fun, but making the 2,550th dinner is heroic.

It's also impossible to make every decision perfectly. In an uncertain world with limited time, we must pick a few issues worthy of serious thought. *Should we skip her to the next grade? Does he feel feverish to you? Are the twins old enough for hockey?* Raising kids is a real-time sport, so many choices have to be made with neither data nor analysis. Arguing carrots versus peas as the dinner vegetable rarely makes my list.

When you put on your product hat (or apron), you'll need to focus your thinking time on what's truly important. At the top of

your menu is a business model built around customer requirements, pricing and competition. Even though this will **never** be
completed to your satisfaction, you'll eventually have to serve it.
Dithering won't get food on the table or software out the door.
(Sometimes the potatoes may taste a little odd.)

SETTING LIMITS IS IMPORTANT (AND DIFFICULT)

Modeling the right kinds of behavior – at the right stages of development – is an art and a science. We want to set ground rules first,
then build on them as our children grow. **No hitting**. **Keep your
clothes on in public**. **We'll read one story before bedtime**. **Don't
touch the steering wheel**. Life is complicated, though, and every
rule has its exception. Lots of parents wrestle with one-time exceptions that instantly reset boundaries. [Remember "*you can stay up
a half hour later tonight, but tomorrow night you have to be in bed
by 8:30PM*" and "*if you really don't feel well enough to go to school
today...*"?] Creating clear policies and deciding when to break
them is nerve-wracking.

Product managers face this daily dilemma with sales teams
(who bring in the revenue that pays our salaries). Moments after
we've carefully defined precisely what we sell and how it's priced,
we're approached with requests for special discounts or unique
packaging or custom features. No exception ever stays a secret,
however: other customers and resellers **always** find out about one-
time deals, so exceptions are really new policies. Yet life demands
flexibility. Our role is to set reasonable thresholds and stay open-
minded. ("*For deals over $100,000 or in these two new markets...*")

Waffling on your policies has longer-term costs. Sales teams and customers learn to "game" your system, describing their special situations to fit your new rules. You're also encouraging them to bring you other kinds of exceptions on the hopes that you'll relax other limits. ("*Here's why this deal is strategic...*") Every parent knows: never let your teenager realize that everything is negotiable.

 ## SOUND BYTE

Great product managers develop an emotional relationship with their products. Like first-time parents, they learn to nurture their products, plan for the future, and make decisions every day with limited experience. **Don't be afraid to commit**. Once you're cleaned up a few dirty MRDs and sent your firstborn off to revenue, there are many more products at your company hoping to be adopted.

Early Selling: Thoroughbreds and Explorers

SEPTEMBER 2002

S tart-up selling is different from selling established products. It includes navigating new product waters and locating islands of early adopters—and calls for different skills than classic quarter-driven account selling. Knowing which you need is critical. (I've seen organizations repeatedly hire the wrong sales force, with terrible results.)

I divide sales teams into thoroughbreds (race horses) and explorers. **Thoroughbreds** outrun the competition along smooth paths by selling well-understood products. **Explorers** hike rough terrain to discover early customers. It's important to know the lay of the land when picking your team.

So, which of these two sounds more like your situation?

- **Surveying the territory:** So far, your first three customers have three unique uses for your product. They have nothing in common except demands for free consulting. You need to invent a market map, define the competitive landscape, and position your product.

    or

- **Starting the quarterly quota race:** You've closed a few dozen deals, have a good description of target customers, and are building a consistent sales process. You can sort mainstream opportunities from dead-end tributaries. Boosting deal size and shortening sales cycle are key goals.

Clearly, the first organization needs to discover a market and find repeatable product solutions. The second organization wants to run ahead of the competition, arriving first to dominate its marketplace. Now, let's match these organizations against their broad choices for sales teams.

THOROUGHBREDS

Top sales people at established companies already think of themselves as thoroughbreds. I agree. So what can we learn about salespeople from racehorses?

- *Without them, racing wouldn't exist.*
- *They are very expensive, but the best earn millions.*
- *They are great at what they do: running like the wind for 1 and 1/4 miles. They don't plough or blaze trails.*
- *They need controlled conditions. Champions don't run on rocky, uneven, badly maintained tracks.*
- *They need a big support staff.*
- *If you have too many thoroughbreds or too few races, they have to run against each other.*

Likewise, top sales people with established companies get top-tier comp packages and live for the end-of-quarter adrenaline rush. They are always well groomed (and wear expensive shoes). Most expect the supporting team to provide a complete selling environment: leads, collateral, awareness, pricing, competitive knockoffs, demo units, pre-sales consulting. You'd love to hire a winner with specific experience on your terrain (e.g. mid-market CRM for automotive). And in the President's Circle, they hold up the trophy on behalf of the whole team.

Warning: don't fill a stable with top sales people before you can afford them. You'll need a repeatable sales process and receptive market to pay for the oats.

EXPLORERS

So, some companies are not ready for herds of thoroughbreds. They don't know the right customer segments or killer application. Perhaps some vertical markets will turn out to be quicksand, and others rich with hidden minerals. These companies need a few sales explorers to map the customer terrain and find a path to success.

When Lewis & Clark set out in 1804 to explore the Western US, they had no map. Thomas Jefferson provided start-up capital and staffing, but no guidance *en route*. What can we learn about selling from this?

- *Lewis & Clark had a mission, but changed tactics and paths frequently.*

- *Getting lost was expected. Discovery was hard to schedule.*

- *They carried everything with them. Solutions were custom-crafted with no help from Washington.*

- *The long, unpredictable journey favored a mix of skills, backgrounds and outlook.*

- *This was a long-term commitment. Replacing team members was not easy.*

Early-stage sales champions have to help find the destination en route. Many discover customer opportunities that Marketing missed. They are comfortable with muddy boots, uncertain sales cycles and changes in product message. Explorers sort prospects early to keep focused on the few with real potential. In partnership with Marketing and Engineering, they keep reconfiguring the available product.

Since the destination isn't yet clear, most explorers have broad industry experience. Someone who's sold Manufacturing ERP as well as channel-driven SME networking gear (or hospital systems or security services...) is a great asset. There's time later to find market-specific stallions.

SOUND BYTE

Consider the maturity of your market when choosing early-stage sales people. Changing explorers into thoroughbreds is difficult, and the reverse nearly impossible.

Burning Your Boats

DECEMBER 2006

I spent 2006 consulting to small tech companies, including seven months as an interim executive. I also *nearly* co-founded a start-up. At year-end, though, I had chosen not to found a new company or join a fledgling venture. This brings to mind discussions of commitment and "burning your boats."

A HISTORICAL DIGRESSION

Hernán Cortés sailed to Mexico in 1519, intent on conquering the Aztecs and claiming their gold for Spain. He landed at Tabasco with 400 soldiers and 15 horses. Worried that his troops might sail back to Spain without him, he ordered his ships burned. This meant that Cortés' conquistadors would have to subdue the locals before they could build fresh boats and return home.

"Burning your boats" has become a well-traveled business metaphor, representing daring and unwavering commitment to an objective. It's an especially attractive concept for big, stagnant companies lacking risk-taking and a focus on customers. (Tom Peters notes that a *"little boat burning would do many enterprises a world of good"*.) Every big organization needs an occasional motivating kick in the org chart.

Of course, history suffers from selection bias: we mostly read about the winners and their daring exploits. Cortés was *right* to burn his boats, perhaps even *brilliant*, since he then led his men to conquest and riches. We assign his success to vision and machismo and strategic thinking – not luck. Emulating him means finding ways to burn our own boats.

It's rarer to hear about Pánfilo de Narváez, who led five Spanish ships and 700 men to conquer Florida eight years later. Narváez ran into natives willing to defend their territory. Result: no gold, no conquest, and only four members of his expedition survived. An unfortunate choice of target markets, since some shot back.

BACK TO START-UPS...

As entrepreneurs, we also have a strong "selection bias." It's well known that the vast majority of new companies fail, and continue to fail at each stage of development. Among thousands of new ventures, only 35 tech companies went public in 2006—the same number as in 2005. But *we* have a winning combination: *our* concept is more compelling; our team is smarter; our investors more experienced and better connected. We've learned from the mistakes of others. Failure is not an option.

The business press reinforces this impression of inevitable success. Fortune and Business 2.0 love underdog stories of scrappy twenty-somethings turning dreams into gold. (*"You can be the next YouTube millionaire if you have enough vision and machismo and risk-seeking brilliance. Just think big and add a cupful of venture money to prove your concept."*)

Unlike 16th century conquest, starting a company doesn't literally risk life and limb. It *does* represent a very serious commitment. Of time. And money. And heart. And prestige. And missed opportunities. Starting or joining an early-stage company is about making an **exclusive choice**: to stop exploring the coastline and choose one cove where you'll anchor for the next few years. During 2006, I passed on several early-stage opportunities and instead chose to keep sailing.

So, here are three things to consider before burning your boats *(founding or joining a brand-new start-up)*:

1. **Is this the right port?** In company terms, is this a market worth exploring with potential customers who need your product/ service? Some investigation before boat-burning is always good: find a few potential buyers and test your new concept. Is there gold in this particular jungle, or just mosquitoes?

2. **Do you have the right crew?** New ventures are very hard work, emotionally challenging, and demand a range of skills. Who is your natural leader, and will everyone else follow? When will you need to expand the management team? By the way, a few start-up veterans are well worth their carrying costs.

3. **Bring enough supplies.** It may take six months to raise initial capital, and another year or two to start generating revenue. Don't let your expedition starve: do a realistic cash projection and plan to spend very frugally. There will be many surprises, most of which will cost money or time.

SOUND BYTE

Do your homework, reconnoiter the coastline, and remember that you'll be living in this market for a long time. Then, when you're ready... burn your boats, plant your flag, stake your claim to the riches of El Dorado. And call me if you need a navigator.

[*By the way, there are non-military substitutes for the boat-burning analogy. Try reading this column again, substituting "dating" and "marriage" for "exploring new ports" and "burning your boats." After all, we give our hearts to our start-ups and products...*]

Avoiding the Post-Course Correction

A s early as 1961, Soviet and American space scientists planned for mid-course corrections: those tiny bursts of rocket power designed to keep spacecraft on their trajectories to the Moon, Mars and beyond. With such long voyages, mid-course corrections are crucial to keeping space flights on track with the minimum of effort – and reserving fuel for later adjustments.

The high-tech opposite of this is something I've come to think of as the "**post-course correction**." This is the panicky "oops" moment when your startup realizes – much too late – that its core strategy and assumptions are flawed. In space terms, **you've missed the moon** and don't have enough resources left for dramatic course changes. There's still air in the cabin (*money in the bank*), but little hope of a soft landing.

BUT BUSINESS ISN'T ROCKET SCIENCE

Of course, no young company moves as predictably as the planets. The startup adventure is all about boldly going. It is critical, though, to focus early on the most important choices your company has to make, and take the time to get them right. Some parts of your initial plan are very difficult to change, and the cost of maneuvering grows over time. Here are a few decisions worth getting right:

- **Pick one destination.** Your initial choice of product and customer shapes everything you're about to do, yet many startups keep postponing this decision – hoping that their technology will solve many as-yet-undiscovered problems. But successful companies focus on one opportunity first, knowing that success is built on more than just the underlying technology.

  Imagine how differently you'd design your **company** to make and sell Xbox-style gaming systems for trend-hopping teens versus CAD/CAM animation for automotive. Or pattern-matching chips versus the retina scanners that use them. Or investment advice versus accounting software. (*In space terms, a Mars rover isn't much use on manned missions.*) The shape of your entire company – including your product – changes as you swing from consumers to enterprise, from OEM to systems vendor.

- **Planning comes before launch.** Over and over again, I see companies start their strategic marketing process just weeks ahead of their public product launch. Panicked, they hire PR firms and marketing consultants to create "buzz" and collateral, without clear messages or target customer segments. Strategic marketing happens many months in advance: *who are our customers, how will we reach them, what is our pricing, how will the competition react?* Successful marketers have done most of their work before the final count-down.

- **Raise more money than you need.** Rockets burn fuel, startups burn cash. Since every company has crises and delays, try to keep a buffer. The best time to ask your investors for more money is before you need it.

That leaves lots of tactical decisions to make during the flight. Most companies will change logos and taglines several times, and shift channel strategies as their markets mature. Customers will keep teaching us which features and benefits matter the most. New technologies create new opportunities. Focus early on the stickiest decisions, freeing up time later for smaller stuff. *In space terms, the overall trajectory is more critical than a few of the scientific experiments along for the ride.*

HOUSTON, WE HAVE A PROBLEM

What does a post-course correction look like? From the dozen I've seen, there's a mad scramble for new market segments and alternative pricing strategies. (*"Do you think we can sell this to the military?" "What about a subscription model instead of package pricing?" "Selling direct to small businesses is too expensive: are there any channels we can sign up?"*) While any of these might be a wise choice, there's little time to decide and execute.

More specifically, this mixes two long-term planning problems. First, post-course correction ideas usually move the company from markets it understand to markets it doesn't. (*For instance,*

CompUSA's acquisition of The Good Guys helped them learn that consumer electronics is different from retail computers, but equally tough to compete in.) Second, it takes time to plan and execute a shift in target markets. If the doors are closing in 60 days, it's too late to reposition the company. Check your trajectory often in case you need to re-think markets or products.

SOUND BYTE

You face some difficult decisions very early in the life of your company. It's worth spending time **now** to choose carefully, because course corrections get more expensive the longer you wait. Once you've missed the moon, it's nearly impossible to land your venture safely.

Why are there Serial Entrepreneurs?

FEBRUARY 2004

F rom the outside, it might seem that joining a fledgling start-up should only be about economics and the big payoff: the popular business press always has stories of farsighted technologists, instant millionaires, and thirty-somethings coping with Sudden Wealth Syndrome. And there are certainly enough folks in the Valley who have made it that most of us know one.

This strikes me as too narrow a view, though - and leaves out the important emotional aspects of start-ups. Deep into my fourth adventure, I'm less occupied by eventual exit strategies than by the day-to-day challenge of managing chaotic growth.

If getting rich were the only motivation for joining a new venture, there would be a steady migration of one-time "winners" leaving Silicon Valley to buy Napa wineries. Instead, I see teams from **successful as well as failed** start-ups throwing themselves into new ventures again and again – reinventing themselves and reinvesting their time in yet another dream. Rather than an end goal, this seems much more of a lifestyle, an addiction, an ongoing creative cycle.

RUNNING THE NUMBERS

First, a few dispassionate statistics: most proto-companies never get past the "idea" stage, with 90%+ closing without ever getting funded. These consume months (years) of unpaid work and late nights from their founders, with very few getting a first product to market. Among companies that raise first-round venture money, more than half shut their doors and return nothing to founders or investors. The small fraction of "successful" companies – those that achieve a soft landing and pay back their investors – are mostly acquired for their intellectual property. There were only 69 IPOs in the last half of 2003, with average value of $196M.

All this is a round-about way of saying that the odds of any particular start-up delivering serious money are quite slim. *Even* with a great team. *And* on-schedule product delivery. *And* good market timing. On top of that, life-altering wealth is only possible for founders, executives, and the first handful of employees.

RATIONALIZING OUR CHOICES

Why lay out such a grim picture? I'm looking for other motives. Silicon Valley seems to be fueled by more than simple greed. Here's an assortment of motivations and rationales: perhaps a few will feel familiar to you. After all, none of us is single-minded or purely rational....

- **Gambler's Fallacy.** The odds don't apply to *me*. I'm much smarter, see the market more clearly, and can form the best team in this new space. My VC contacts will jump at the chance to fund us, for "first mover" advantage. Our founders have all formed companies before, so we've made our mistakes elsewhere. (*Do you know any founder who doesn't truly believe this?*)

- **I *won't* work for big companies anymore.** The big rush of a start-up is sitting face-to-face with customers and trying to solve their problems. There's a scramble of activity focused on actual results, not an internal negotiation among business units and multilayered functional organizations. My little team can build and ship a solution in 4 months by avoiding the 18 months of budget reviews and executive sponsorships and trade-offs that are inevitable in a 1000 person company.

- **I *can't* work for big companies anymore.** After a couple of start-ups, I've lost the patience, process view, and polite attitude that bigger companies demand. My urgent need to make something (*anything!*) happen leaves me unable to sit through a two-hour budget meeting. I can't resynch my "fix it today" expectations with the long-term planning of a broader organization.

- **It's not the company, but the work.** My sense of belonging is to my functional team, not to this particular start-up: I'm a journeyman tech writer (QA engineer, channel sales manager, product marketer) rather than a long-term employee. Being at a one-product company means that I'll have fewer reorganizations and interruptions, since we have only one thing to build. If this company evaporates, our entire crew will move to the next start-up – and we can pick up where we left off. (*This might be like the medieval stone masons: when one cathedral was finished, they packed their tools and walked down the road to the next cathedral-in-progress.*)

- **Big companies are no longer hiring.** Since exiting HP or Sun or Oracle or SGI a couple of startups ago, there's no way back. There's no stability to be found in the Valley, and I might as well have some upside. Over the course of a career, I'm certain to be at one start-up that makes me a bundle. What's the alternative?

- **The valley is really one big company already**, just broken into many parts. There are partnerships, zaibatsus, ecosystems and old-boy networks that substitute for much of the big company structure. If I think of business development as the modern replacement for departmental politics, everything looks the same as before. My last few failed start-ups form a terrific alumni network.

- **Start-ups are addictive**. "*Hi, my name is Rich and I'm hooked. I was clean for two years, but somehow fell in with another venture-backed company...*" Perhaps all of our rationales are irrelevant, and we just crave the daily confusion and adrenaline. Smart folks can eventually justify any behavior.

And so on. Perhaps one of these strikes home. Or, if I've missed your special rationale for being part of a jumbled experiment, please let me know. There's probably a twelve-step program here that a clever entrepreneur can shorten to four steps – and ship in 1/3 the time.

SOUND BYTE

Being part of a start-up is about more than get-rich-quick dreams. It's an emotional commitment to a hurried, harried, adrenaline-driven way of working. For those who can cope, it seems oddly addictive.

Owning the Gap

P roduct managers are usually the people who "own the gap" for their specific products: identifying all of the missing or incomplete features and services and supporting processes that customers need for a successfully experience. This discussion is about elevating that concept to the product executive, who should be looking for systemic problems in the company's end-to-end production cycle.

OWNING THE PRODUCT GAP

Customers don't just buy a fragmentary bit of software functionality or a solitary stick of technology hardware. They are trying to solve some problem with the least amount of effort and confusion. Good product managers are constantly watching for ways to meet this overall need - helping the customer actually get something done - as well as the atomic details of their products. Classic examples of product gaps include:

- Missing software drivers (or connectors or fonts or adapters or batteries) not supplied with the base product
- Tech support phone systems that demand a product serial number before letting the caller get help

- Very restrictive system requirements (``*must have XP Service Pack 2*'') that most users don't have and won't notice on the point-of-sale package
- Confusingly similar product names with poorly differentiated features
- Installation help files that aren't visible until after a successful installation

And so on. An old piece of mine about software bills of materials (``*Avoiding a Ticking B-O-M*'') recaps this thought. In a well-run organization, a product manager **identifies and owns her product gaps until she is able to get some responsible department to take them back**.

Notice that a ground-level product manager is doing his best to find these gaps one at a time, through common sense and clear thinking and frustrated customer emails. The goal is to get one more product out the door in working order, correctly packaged and labeled, so that buyers can put it into action.

This "personal effort" does not address system-wide questions, though. Are product managers in various groups seeing the same kinds of problems? Are there chronic outbreaks of similar customer complaints? How can we improve the process?

OWNING THE ORGANIZATIONAL GAP

Product managers don't live in a vacuum. They are part of some broader organization with its own challenges and problems. Ideally, they report up through a management chain that wants them to succeed, and wants the company to make money by shipping great products. The VP of Product Management (or similar executive) needs to find ways of helping the company succeed at the overall task of designing and shipping things for revenue.

I'd propose three kinds of gaps that the product executive owns:

1. **Resource gaps.** When another department is understaffed or overwhelmed, someone needs to be their champion. Vocally supporting these departments at the executive level is a good way to make progress. For instance, most companies short-change and understaff QA... the folks tasked with making sure that products are actually installable, bugs are fixed, and features remotely resemble brochures. QA is at the heart of end user satisfaction, customer references, and effective sales engineers. Inevitably, though, as schedules slip, delivery dates remain fixed by cutting QA time.

   Individual PMs know where the staffing gaps are, but can't fix the problem locally. Product executives should be lobbying on their behalf for real schedules and sufficient resources to meet them. (The same issue comes up in Technical Support, which should be a source of great customer input but is often just a cost center.)

2. **Incentive Gaps.** Lots of companies have created systems that reward or excuse bad behavior. Just as PMs think deeply about how customer behavior shifts with different pricing models, a product executive needs to be watching for perverse organizational incentives.

   A small version of this is the sales compensation plan. If reps are getting bonuses to bring in beta/pilot accounts, they will - but won't spend time qualifying these accounts as revenue customers. Similarly, if reps are paid a lot more for direct selling than channel sales, you should expect dozens of reasons why important deals need to be sold direct. Sales reps do what you pay them to do (not necessarily what you *want* them to do).

A bigger example is where all of the company's executives get bonuses if Product X ships before year end. To no one's surprise, the EVPs all decide on December 24th that Beta 1 can go to revenue customers. So that major accounts don't get into trouble, the VP Sales approves all shipments personally. Of course, the time to lobby against shipment bonuses is at the **beginning** of the project. A savvy Product Management VP will propose an alternate bonus, to be paid when we get our first three customer references.

3. **Technology gaps.** Sometimes, individual business units don't see the commonality of their requirements. They may all face the same competitor, or be licensing technology from the same supplier. Individual PMs are heads-down, so have trouble seeing the broader context. The product executive should arrange for periodic forums where all PMs can share (commiserate) and put the puzzle together. You may find some interesting cross-divisional opportunities.

Notice that all three of these are organizational issues, not purely technical issues. The solutions usually require executive teams to cooperate on decisions, allocate resources, align compensation plans, and generally tell their departments to help each other. Thus the VP Product Management needs to be shaping the organization at this level, the same way that individual product managers are driving grass-roots product efforts.

SOUND BYTE

It's easy to be hypnotized by the products themselves, but success is a mix of organizations and implementation and process. Product executives need to work organizational issues, and PMs need to ask them for that help.

Girls Getting a Head Start (-Up)

MAY 2004

Most founders of VC-backed start-ups tend toward technical degrees, MBAs and forty-something gray hair - with a strong male bias. Here in the heart of Silicon Valley, though, there's a group of seventh-grade girls who are doing it all: writing business plans, raising venture capital, manufacturing products, and running their own profitable companies. Ten years from now, you may be working for one of them.

The Girls' Middle School (**www.girlsms.org**) has a required full-year course in Entrepreneurship where all of the girls form companies, design products, and build defensible business plans. The highlight of the first half-year was a pitch night for actual Sand Hill VCs to get their start-up capital, complete with PowerPoint slides and an audience of 300. That started a frenzied six-month selling season for companies that made jewelry, snack foods, fleece clothing, and handbags sewn from recycled juice pouches.

[Full disclosure: I'm related to one of these Young Turks. I was able to watch from the sidelines while they did competitive analysis, computed contribution margins, and sold to sometimes-indifferent buyers. My big challenge was to not help.]

WHAT DID YOU LEARN IN SCHOOL TODAY?

Coming to the end of the year, I asked some of these proto-entre-preneurs what they learned. See if these sound familiar.

1. **Pick your founding team carefully.** Some of the girls were focused and aggressive; others were less organized or preoccu-pied. Keeping on their year-long schedule for business plan-ning, design prototyping, market research and selling took emotional endurance. Each company picked an Operations VP to motivate and coordinate the other officers, with varying results. (Did I work for this start-up in the late 90's?)

2. **Do some early customer research.** Some companies had to switch products early on, after finding that their first product lines didn't sell. Good experience, but the groups who squeezed in some test marketing got a faster start.

3. **Pick sales channels that reach your target customers.** Unsur-prisingly, most of the ten companies made products for teen/tween girls. ("Know your customer.") Finding sales venues was very challenging, however. Outside of school, where do you set up shop to reach teen girls? Malls discourage unlicensed vendors, and supermarkets trend toward adults. The local farmer's market had mixed results. Perhaps eBay?

4. **Managing to the numbers is hard.** None of these young execs had experience projecting sales or cost-of-goods. Eight months later, they had a sharper sense of their ventures' inputs and outputs. Like all of the start-ups I've seen, teams had to scram-ble and re-plan as they reached the market.

5. **Lean on experience.** Each team had two adult coaches, meet-ing weekly on deliverables and progress. The coaches pro-vided sage advice, particularly on "intracompany dynamics."

(That's a polite phrase for staying focused and working together.) Pencil in "board of directors" here.

This week, the companies liquidated: inventories cleared, investors and employees paid, charitable donations made. Each team closed its project with a final VC meeting.

BOOT CAMP IN SENSIBLE SHOES

This was experiential learning, not just an afternoon's discussion. Groups had to live with their choices. Hard to build your product? **Redesign it.** Sales event didn't draw a crowd? **Try somewhere else.** Lost the cash box? **Search like crazy, or you can't pay back your investors.** A stark contrast with many of the one-session cases I read at Stanford. (*"You are the CEO of a major manufacturer..."*)

For the fifth year, the program has been run by two women steeped in the Silicon Valley ethos: an engineer and an attorney who have each founded companies. They've provided not only a serious hands-on curriculum, but unmistakable role models. The subtext is clear: with or without boys, these girls are getting down to business.

SOUND BYTE

Everyone's first start-up is about immersion and first-hand learning. You don't need a driver's license (or a beard) to dive in.

Organizing your Organization

People are More Important than Products

Companies are made up of people, and people are complicated.
We left-brained folks like to draw organizational charts with clear
titles and lots of symmetry – but know that individuals matter. People won't stay in the boxes we assign them.

As the non-hierarchical leaders of matrixed teams, product managers need to understand how people think and how they act. We
are constantly tuning our own styles to move product teams
along: coaxing, rationalizing, motivating, berating, escalating,
negotiating, twiddling our thumbs to contain our rampant impa-
tience, occasionally tattling to executives. Mix in some customer
meetings (listening, arguing, selling, and small bursts of blatant
customer sucking-up) and you have the emotional range of an
average PM's day.

It's not surprise, then, that great PMs worship their copies of Steven
Kerr's "On the Folly of Rewarding A...[2]" This 1975 paper reminds us
that people do what we **reward** them to do – not what we **want**
them to do – and applies widely to internal organizations as well
as customers and prospects. This mental model is especially
handy as you manipulate organizations (reward systems, pricing
models, commission plans, bonus structures, unsolicited thank-
yous copied to Management) to nudge people in the right direction.

Even if world doesn't always work this way, it makes me feel better to believe it. This section, then, is about the semi-rational relationship between product managers and organizations: thinking
through our own needs and motivations while we lobby to get better products built faster.

---

2. The Academy of Management Journal, Vol. 18, No. 4, 769-783.
    Dec., 1975. "On the Folly of Rewarding A, While Hoping for B," Ste-
    ven Kerr Ohio State University.

Where Should PM Report?

OCTOBER 2003

A perennial problem for Product Management (PM) is finding the right organizational home. In companies large enough to have a PM department, it has a tendency to oscillate between Marketing and Engineering. Two root causes for this are role confusion and organizational distance. Let's walk through each in turn, while trying to map a PM's place in the grand scheme.

WHAT'S IN A TITLE?

Most companies have very few Product Managers, and their actual jobs vary widely. Typically, without enough PMs to form a separate department, these lonely few work in an organization that doesn't understand them. So, a first step would be to define a couple of the roles that are not Product Management, and tighten up the job boundaries. *(This is my ideal division of labor. Others are welcome to object.)*

Program Manager[3], aka Project Manager: This is the person who owns Engineering's master PERT chart. She is responsible for

---

3. With the move to Agile, we've seen a proliferation of new titles. This adds significant confusion, since good Scrum Masters meet very similar (or identical) needs as good project managers. The Scrum Alliance's creation of "product owner" muddies this further, since product owners cover a small subset of a product manager's role and are not actually responsible for the success of products. They may own an iteration, but don't own a product or release or determinant of market success.

knowing the status and timeline for every phase review, feature, manual, QA cycle, code check-in, and step in the release process. The best program manager can tell you to the day how late your software project will be. A master of resource allocation, she will present complex trade-offs within the project. *("If we QA the external interface before the database routines, we can start writing the user guide nine days earlier but may slip the synchronization feature...")*

Typically, the Program Manager offers up difficult choices to someone outside Engineering, since these choices will have customer impact and political ramifications.

Product Marketer: This is someone in Marketing who must make your products sound attractive. His goal is to help Sales sell more stuff. This often includes a daily battle to make the competition look weak, and to justify the "right" answers on customer RFPs. In the hunt for revenue, it's hard to stay pure or objective - and easy to believe in the customer's ability to be fooled. Trading away the future for the present is irresistible. The best product marketers know how to make lemonade out of under-ripe products.

What's missing between these two roles is a decision-making role. **The Product Manager is the brave soul who has to balance competing interests and take a stand.** In the midst of uncertainty and unpredictable outcomes, the PM has to drive choices every day. In the course of a morning, a good PM will have to weigh in on:

- Our Omaha account team says they can sell 25 units if we commit to a LINUX port for January. They need an answer before Noon.

- Double-byte Chinese character support is behind schedule. Should we delay final shipment or push this feature to the next maintenance release? What's the revenue impact?
- Which of these ten bugs are show-stoppers?
- Citibank wants a look at our unpublished internal interfaces.
- What if we bundle all three of these products together and increase the price?
- Let's save money by shipping manuals on CD only, and not including hard copy manuals.

Often, the PM is a proxy for the customer. This means taking positions of long-term benefit to the company (e.g. happy reference accounts) instead of short-term ones (e.g. shipping partially tested products).

Ideally, you want your PM to be both **right** and **decisive**. It may take years to find out if a decision was right, but indecisiveness can freeze up an entire organization. A great PM recognizes the important few decisions worthy of serious analysis – and plows through the rest.

David Thompson, a manager of mine at iPass, taught me that executives are paid to make decisions: a productive day must include least one decision. Meetings, emails, discussions, forecast reviews and brainstorming are secondary to making decisions that drive action. It's easy to be distracted by the minutiae of business, or by analysis paralysis.

So, we've defined the ideal PM: an experienced, decisive driver who understands the customer enough to make complex trade-offs. Now we can tackle the second half of the problem: which organization should "own" product management?

THE PENDULUM SWINGS

Perhaps that's the wrong question. I've seen organizations go through an annual cycle: moving PMs into Engineering from Marketing in Year 1, then back into Marketing from Engineering in Year 2. If there were a perfect answer to PM reporting structures, we'd all have found it by now. *(Consider diet books. If any truly offered a solution, we'd all be thin.)* Instead, consider the failures that drive this organizational lurch.

When PMs sit in Engineering, they spend their time with engineers. Days are filled with detailed discussion of bugs, development priorities, release trains, and software bundling. **Especially in the absence of Program Managers**, PMs dive deeper and deeper into the product creation process. This leads to technically good products, but a marketing failure.

Engineering PMs know their features very well, but are weak on benefits and sales materials. They impress technical users at conferences, but don't know how customers are using their products. They under-invest in competitive analysis and a compelling high-level story. Too much steak and not enough sizzle.

After a year of this, the Marketing VP and Sales VP organize a hostile take-over. Ignoring the objections of Engineering, product managers are moved into Marketing and relocated next to Sales. Suddenly, PMs are spending more time with customers and sales teams, working harder on messages, and educating the field force. They have more time to stalk the competition, writing seemingly neutral white papers to slant public opinion.

Within a quarter or two, though, Engineering is starting to protest. Product requirements now lack detail, development trade-offs are starting to bog down, and engineers are spending valuable time briefing customers. PMs are falling out of touch with schedules and upcoming features. Without daily meetings in Engineering, PMs are becoming "all hat and no cattle." Here comes the Engineering VP with a new org chart in her hand.

WHAT'S A PM TO DO?

It's critical to recognize that product management is an interstitial role, a bridging function between Marketing/Sales and Engineering. PMs own the organizational gap, since they need to deliver real solutions to the customer.

Letting the pendulum swing too far toward either side is a failure. On the westward loop (toward Engineering), PMs must work extra hard to spend time with customers and sales teams. This lets them use the most powerful phrase ever uttered in a lab: *"Here's what this customer told me..."*

On the eastbound swing back to Marketing, PMs need to find informal time to hang with the techies. This is outside the stultifying weekly status meetings, or the "everything is still on schedule" nod from the VP Development. Staying fresh with the technology keeps them informed, generates good ideas, and reinforces a sense of the possible. It's time to replace your product manager when she can no longer sort good ideas from bad. *("What about adding teleportation to our warehouse management software?")*

Said another way, Product Management never really reports up through one function. Good PMs own long-term decisions that routinely cross the artificial organizational boundaries. By representing customers instead of departments, PMs are a unifying force in a divided model.

SOUND BYTE

When reporting up through Engineering, PMs need to think like marketers. When in Marketing, like engineers. And keep those boxes handy, because another reorganization is coming soon.

The Roadmap Less Traveled

JULY 2003

Every tech start-up struggles to create a roadmap: that short set of PowerPoint slides which defines the next six quarters of updates, minor releases and important advances. Since product managers strive for clarity, having a product roadmap is a critical communications tool. However...

- Sales is constantly pressing for roadmaps that show what today's customer requires, including a committed delivery date. "*Once we close the deal, we can figure out how to build what's missing.*"

- Yet Engineering uses the roadmap as a target for product deliveries. Everything on the chart is a hoped-for objective; anything missing has been definitively dropped.

Therefore, we are talking about two distinct roadmaps with non-overlapping uses. Referring to both as "*the* product roadmap" creates endless confusion.

WHAT'S IN A NAME?

The (less traveled) road to clarity starts with precise nomenclature, so let's first consider the "**engineering roadmap**." You may have also called this beast the "release plan" or the "internal schedule" or the "development calendar." Fundamentally, it captures our technical **aspirations**: what we hope will happen.

This engineering roadmap is for **internal use only**. It's designed to help the technical team fit each project into an overall release process - coding, QA, beta testing and customer shipment - and drive staff assignments. Every work item must be included; otherwise it will be dropped, de-emphasized, or assumed away. Engineering managers need to show sustaining tasks as well, to justify headcount and budgets within the development group.

None of this would matter if most technical projects finished on time. Sadly, 'taint so. (*In 1995, I brought out a software product on time, on budget, and on spec. Never before and never since.*) What happens when things are late? Engineering managers dance through a complex series of postponements, reduced features, QA shrinkages, shortened betas, and redefinitions of success. In other words, **the current engineering roadmap is always the high water mark**. Things will never again be as good as they are today.

ALONG THE OTHER PATH...

Customers, of course, believe in product planning. They will hold your sales person at invoice-point and demand to see your current roadmap. (Here, we mean something completely different: the "**public roadmap**" or "customer NDA plan" or "analyst briefing chart.")

Knowing that dates shift and specific functions are always at risk, a Product Manager should craft a public roadmap that is long on vision and light on details. Near-term projects will have much more precision than next year's SWAGs. Delivery dates should be a quarter later than engineering dates, anticipating slippage.

Enterprise customers *should* understand (but please don't tell them during an important meeting) that all projects more than 6 months away are subject to change. *"Time-from-now"* is a good measure of speculative risk. Still, you need a multi-year story about product directions to appear strategic. Keep it light and simple! When you can, avoid customizing roadmaps for several key prospects along incompatible dimensions. The smart ones will keep copies of your presentation, and ask very pointed questions as their favorite items fail to ship.

TELL THEM WHAT THEY WANT TO HEAR?

In my experience, some softly phrased honesty nourishes relationships with serious customers. (*"That's a great suggestion, but it would have a lot of implementation risk. Let me tell you why, and explore other ways that we might address your business requirements."*) Often, savvy customers demand a face-to-face roadmap discussion with product managers to get closer to R&D's reality, and sidestep your sales team's natural optimism. An hour with someone who can explain tough trade-offs is a way for thoughtful customers to make informed decisions.

How can you say "no" to a customer? Take a note from our Japanese colleagues, who have perfected the fine art of gentle discouragement. In Tokyo, an audible breath through the teeth and *"that could be very difficult"* is one polite way of refusing a request. Here in the US, product managers might say "that's on our roadmap, but we are still working on scheduling and priorities." Another favorite placeholder is "that's a great idea! Let me review it with our architects and see where it will fit in our plan."

SOUND BYTE

Engineering roadmaps and public release plans are related – but are not the same item. When you hear that "we need a roadmap slide," consider responding with a brief interrogation: internal or external? NDA or public pre-sentation? Major deal closer or just fishing?

I'd consider two or three distinct (*and distinctly named*) documents: a public roadmap for use with press, analysts and prospects; a Key Customer roadmap, used strictly under NDA when Product Management is present; and a Development calendar for staffing, planning and execu-tive buy-in. Getting agreement and maintaining these is hard work.

Crowding Out Tech Support

There's been a lot of discussion in the blogosphere and popular press about "crowdsourcing" -- empowering crowds of amateurs to do tasks previously done by professionals. This creates the next trendy opportunity for companies to offload parts of themselves onto the market.

Tech Support (aka Customer Support) is on many executives' lists of outsource-able functions. I've been talking with Tech Support teams at several startups, however, and see real value in a dedicated team that helps customers love you. Here's my contrarian view on getting more out of support teams.

FIRST, SOME BACKGROUND

Tech Support (Customer Support) is the group of live humans helping customers and prospects in active phone and email conversations. They also own online vehicles for customer self-service: FAQs, chat and support blogs. More than any other group, Support serves customers who have already paid money for your products – and whose repeat business is critical to next year's revenue.

Often, though, I see Tech Support ignored, under-equipped, and stuffed into an organizational closet. A cost center, a necessary evil, tasked with answering calls as quickly as possible. New product training is an afterthought, metrics are missing, and promotion into better-paying positions is rare. *A perfect opportunity for outsourcing, offshoring or crowdsourcing.*

This approach is built on hidden assumptions that [1] our products are perfect, [2] all customers will support themselves online, and [3] customers will still happily recommend our products even if we treat them badly. **Wrong on all counts.**

In my experience, making Support a strategic asset takes a combination of **organizational planning, good tools,** and **product management thinking**. Let's grapple with each in turn...

AN ORGANIZATIONAL HOME

Tech Support usually reports up through Engineering. Unfortunately, a lot of Support requests sound to engineers like criticism: *"our customers are having trouble installing the new graphics application"* or *"the UI is confusing."* Engineering has plenty to fix without new problems from Support, so naturally ignores what it can. *(Ask someone in QA what reaction she gets when filing new bug reports.)*

Another approach is to move Support into the Sales organization. This tends to co-opt Support into a tele-selling role, pushing service contract renewals and paid upgrades, when they should be concentrating on understanding and pacifying upset customers.

I've seen some good alternatives: Splunk has rolled Support under Product Management, so that fresh customer input flows right into PM. Cemaphore has Tech Support included in a broader Operations group alongside IT, and has Support do product acceptance testing. Regardless of its location, Tech Support needs some executive help to avoid obscurity.

TOOLS OF THE TRADE

Once the team has a home, don't forget some basic tools. Like the shoemaker's barefoot children, Tech Support teams at tech companies often lack necessities:

- **Customer information.** You don't need a fancy CRM system. In fact, research suggests that customers really want to talk with engaged and empowered employees who can actually address problems... which CRM systems can undermine. Double points if you can tell whose support contract needs renewal.

- **A case tracking system.** Not to be confused with CRM systems, these capture details about customers and problems. A good Case Tracking System can help you identify trends, patterns and root causes of issues. FYI, PostIt® notes are not a good substitute.

- **A few regular metrics.** Once you're tracking each case, start with weekly reporting of case loads, portion of cases closed on the first call, and which products generate the most problems. Don't be seduced into giving bonuses for "fewest minutes spent per customer."

- **Lots of bite-sized product training.** The best Tech Support reps are empathetic and enjoy interacting with customers. If they *"give good phone,"* they are probably bad at sitting still for extended classroom training. Explore product training that takes advantage of multiple media, unplanned down time, or lunch-and-learns for bite-sized product updates.

All of this seems obvious, yet many companies go without. They've failed to find an organizational champion and a systematic view of customer support. Along the way, they've failed to pull corporate-wide value from Tech Support.

Here's where some classic product management skills apply: how do we **think about Support** as a way to improve the company's products and position in the marketplace? Where can we gain advantage from the Support organization we've already paid for?

THINKING LIKE A PRODUCT GUY

Support folks tend to be technical, straightforward, and headsdown. Few understand the non-technical challenges of product planning, and fewer have spent much time with Product Managers. Injecting a little product thinking can yield some great results.

Imagine, then, a monthly sit-down with product management and technical support, where both teams grapple with the "top ten" support list. Starting with reports of actual case loads, everyone can learn by sorting issues into distinct categories.

Note that the way we propose to fix a problem depends on the category we assign it to: communications problems are solved by communicating better; software problems are fixed with new releases. Putting problems in the wrong bucket leads to wrong-headed solutions.

Here's an assortment from a recent Support/Product Mgmt triage session:

- **Customers Can't Find the Answer.** For instance, just after you ship a new software version, you should expect lots of *"what's your upgrade policy"* inquiries. Before the next launch, consider putting the upgrade policy at the top of your FAQ page *and* in the customer newsletter *and* on your home page *and* in email blasts to licensees.

- **Customers Can't Find the *Feature*.** When users have trouble locating a menu item or function that's already in your product, you probably have a UI or naming problem. For instance, if Tech Support is constantly telling customers that your version of Mail Merge is called "Customized Letter Generator," then perhaps you should change its name. *And* list it under the Tools menu. *And* cross-index both names in your help files.

- **Our software crashes.** A bug. Get it fixed. No excuses.

- **Positioning a Non-Feature.** The product team may already have decided not to include a requested feature. Tech Support needs help explaining this. Spend some time on **why** a feature won't be included, and **how** Support should talk about this to customers, with answers like *"Here's an easier way to do the same thing..."* and *"Some good third party products that work well in this situation are..."* and *"We've had some other customers raise concerns about this feature because..."*

- **Policy issues**, such as who gets free upgrades, are the toughest for Tech Support -- callers always have excuses for breaking your company's rules. Set some reasonable rules with minimal red tape. (*"If anyone from our top 50 customers calls and has a valid email address at that company, give them all of the help* *they need. The account manager will clean up any billing issues after the crisis is over.")*

And so on. Figuring out what kind of problem you have is the toughest part of solving it. Together, Support and Product Management can improve products and customer experience.

 SOUND BYTE

Tech Support sounds like something your company should outsource or "crowdsource," but you may instead drive off your customers. Get Support the organizational and strategic help it needs to capture real customer value.

Product Management is Inherently Political

SEPTEMBER 2004

R ecently, I had lunch with a bright young product manager trying to perfect the process for deciding which features to include in his next product release. Skipping past theory about "internal ROI" and other quantitative approaches, we talked about having to choose among the many demands for enhancements from sales teams: that MRDs are only the starting point in an ongoing lobbying campaign for product improvements. In other words, product managers will always have to manage the emotional world of people and internal politics.

FIRST, LET'S SET THE STAGE

As product manager for the next version of TechX, you've collected a nearly infinite list of possible improvements, advances, new features, and architectural repairs. Your goal is to build an orderly list of items, review them with Engineering for size and suitability, then issue a definitive requirements document (MRD or PRD) that formally declares what will be built. Being analytical and a bit compulsive, you think of this as the **end** of a long process, after which Engineering will leap into action.

You've had to make choices from a dissimilar list of potential projects:

- **Customer specials** needed by specific big accounts, even if they are not likely to be of general use to others (more on this later)

- **Broad feature improvements** as demanded by the market, reviews, user groups, and your keen sense of what customers want

- **Internal architectural changes** that will be invisible to customers but are needed for improved quality or longer-term goals

- The occasional **high-profile product bet** anticipating emerging market needs or hoped-for shifts in related technologies

Trade-offs within each group are easy, but across groups are nearly impossible. Part of your job is to balance these different categories so that your next release meets a few needs from each group. (*Does this sound like a state budgeting process?*)

Within each group, you try to draw up rational criteria. Among features demanded by specific customers, you look to your sales teams for revenue commitments and certainties. (*"How big is the deal? Is this the only feature blocking the sale? Can we get a commitment from the customer to buy if we deliver by March 15th?"*) You probably built a deal-specific spreadsheet to track opportunities and likelihoods, which you will need later.

For more general market requests, you poll sales teams and industry analysts. Engineering typically demands a few sacrifices to the gods of architecture, so a few of these make the cut.

In addition, you are trading off time and resources against your overall list. For example, adding a data conversion option will push back the release date by two weeks. Including Voice-over-Telepathy costs five months. Since most engineering schedules run late, you need to negotiate a delivery date that gives you some breathing room. Etc.

Ultimately, an MRD is the culmination of intense negotiations with all parties (engineering, marketing, sales, customers). It represents a compromise based on your best judgment and the facts on hand. Great PMs deliver superior MRDs and also leave each constituent group feeling valued/respected/listened to. After emailing the final MRD to all groups, your team takes you out for a well-deserved celebration. This *feels* like a milestone.

BUT THE FUN HAS JUST STARTED

Nearly immediately, two kinds of problems arise. One is caused by actual changes in the world: shifting customer needs, market trends, product experience, and general evolution. The second is lobbying from the sales teams who did not get their favorite enhancements into your MRD. By making hard choices about which features are in your next release, you've had to postpone other legitimate requests.

A quick aside about your most successful sales teams: they are experts at understanding and influencing how customers make decisions. Faced with customers who want to make rational buying choices using objective criteria, they will cajole, schmooze influencers, rewrite RFPs, promise upcoming features, sponsor golf outings, scrutinize budgets, and generally work to tilt rational decisions in your company's favor. This is **precisely** what makes them so successful and so valuable to your company. And why they take deals away from less aggressive competitors. And why they wield such influence internally.

What should you expect from sales teams that don't get their favorite features committed in your MRD? The same behavior that you've consistently rewarded them for: lobbying Sales executives about the strategic importance of their deals, having customers call you demanding action, rejiggering revenue projections to improve relative ranking, taking you to lunch, asking your boss to send you "into the field" for a week, insisting that one more feature can be shoehorned into the release. You may call this "politics." Sales teams call this "influencing decision-makers to improve the MRD process." Remember that you normally applaud this approach.

Now, we have an analytically-minded product manager beset by account teams trying to reprioritize the MRD. Each sales team has some legitimate argument or new information to present. You would rather be managing the next phase of product delivery than listening politely to ten more pleas for help. How did you find yourself in this situation, and what can you do next time to avoid this trap?

POLITICAL ISSUES REQUIRE POLITICAL SOLUTIONS

Allocating scarce resources always leaves some people dissatisfied, and drives them to escalate complaints or question the decision-making process. This is certainly true of MRDs, which prioritize Engineering's projects and schedules. You can call this "politics" if you like, or "group decision-making" or any handy phrase from the MBA Organizational Behavior handbook. Regardless of the label, even the perfect MRD will leave some of your constituents unhappy. To keep the process moving forward, you need political support for the decision process and your final choices. Generally, I'd suggest this comes out of a pre-negotiation with the head of Sales. Imagine this discussion with your VP of Sales:

- *"If we're going to hit our delivery dates for TechX version 5, we can allocate up to 45 engineering-weeks to one-off enhancements for high profile customers. I need your help to support the most important deals. I've built this spreadsheet of requests, required effort and likely revenue."*

  *"**OK**"*

- *"Looks like we could commit to these 5 special deals for GM, Goldman Sachs, Deutsche Telekom, the Air Force, and Safeway. That leaves 20 other deals uncommitted, including Sloan Kettering and FedEx. Are there any you'd move up the list and replace the ones I chose? After all, I'm just a lowly product guy and not the all-knowing head of Sales."*

  *"**This looks about right. Good job**."*

- *"One other thing I need: those next 20 account teams are going to be pushing you hard to get their enhancements back in. I need your commitment that we won't add any to the list without pulling off one of these 5. If we expand the requirements, the release date will slip and you'll lose several of your top deals."*

"**Hmmm. How about if I go over your list with my regional managers and make sure this is right? We'll get back to you by Monday.**"

- "*Absolutely. You're my customer on this. After your meeting, I'd love your initials at the bottom of my spreadsheet, so that I know I have the right information handy for follow-up discussions...*"

What just happened? You found someone in Sales to help make and confirm decisions, and a defined method for considering changes. When the sales rep covering United Airlines calls you, feel free to explain that her VP of Sales approved the final list. This also sets up a more rational discussion about changing priorities: if FedEx is suddenly more important than Safeway, you can explore the revenue and technical trade-offs involved in swapping their place in the queue. Getting "buy-in" from Sales management means that your choices are more likely to meet Sales' overall goals and revenue objectives.

Of course, this applies to the other key constituents of your MRD: executives in Engineering, Marketing and perhaps Finance or Manufacturing. Having your decisions ratified **now** by future lobbyists will keep things moving.

SOUND BYTE

Product managers are paid to make decisions that have an impact on the broader organization. This makes us part of the internal political process. Rather than ignore this reality, we need to understand how decisions are made and re-made, then design our processes to let the real world help us.

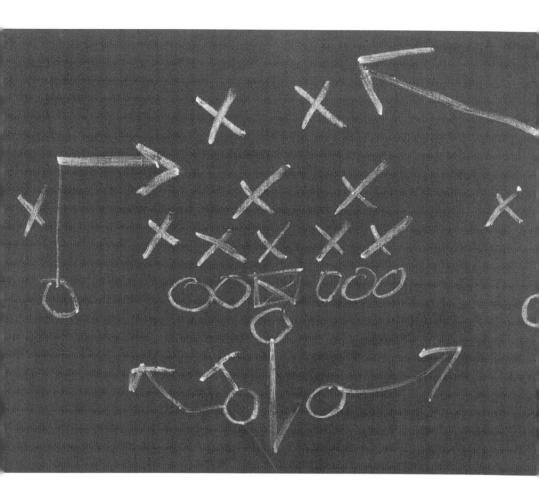

Defensive Processes

FEBRUARY 2005

N ew ventures begin with an entirely empty slate: no products, no customers, no desks, no organization charts, no established procedures for creating value. Only blank pages and empty office space. This is part of the exhilaration, the chance to do things better and more simply than the last time.

Of course, your founding team brings lots of experience: idea about how things get done. As the product champion, you'll almost immediately be defining what your startup makes and how it gets delivered. Generically, "processes".

If you're lucky enough to have joined a winner, things will grow. Quickly. As a startup goes from 15 employees to 40 to 100, there are increasing calls for building repeatable processes. Let's think about creating a few good processes and avoiding ones that add little value.

Generally, I'd break these into two groups:

- **Constructive processes:** how do we get things done? How can we do them better? These include fundamentals like design documents, sales territories, and price lists. No business can function without them.
- **Defensive processes:** how do we avoid making mistakes? Slanted toward control and compliance, these include sign-off

on purchase orders and cross-department review of product readiness.

Of course, both varieties are necessary. An energetic team should be focused mostly on constructive processes – getting something done more quickly and more correctly – with the least effort spent on jumping over self-imposed hurdles. When mistakes are made, though, it's easy to build ever-more-perfect ways of impeding your work.

HOW ABOUT AN EXAMPLE?

First, let's consider some positive, constructive processes that are easily neglected:

- **Bill of Materials.** If your product is even slightly complicated, it helps to know **precisely** what's included. Customers will ask, manufacturing needs to build it, and Engineering should know when all of the pieces are ready. A BoM settles hundreds of seemingly simple questions across the company. The hour spent getting this right is paid back many times over.

- **Support escalation process.** Who should customers call when they have a problem? During what hours? What should your support team do with issues that can't be immediate resolved? If the customer is still unhappy? This doesn't have to be complicated, but needs to be crystal clear.

  I've been on too many calls with frustrated customers who ring every executive at the company – in turn – and demand immediate action from each. Few things are less effective than a swarm of VPs interrupting the real problem solvers for hourly progress reports. Knowing who owns each phase of a problem keeps your team focused on useful activity.

- **Target Segments and Channels.** This seems obvious, but most startups are afraid to focus. Some of the sales force is selling directly to US small businesses, while others are calling on European telecoms resellers. Even if you turn out to be wrong, you should decide on an explicit shift after you've gathered some real market experience.

  It's worth having **one** person in Marketing or Business Development who catches oddball opportunities. Someone to investigate what you're shielding everyone else from.

SEEMS OBVIOUS

You get the idea. In contrast, though, think about the last few minor screw-ups in your company and how managers reacted. Consider these defensive clunkers:

- **Triple-checking customer orders.** A fair portion of incoming orders arrive misconfigured, or have the wrong prices and discounts, or use last quarter's part numbers. Our order admin team doesn't always catch problems, so we've added a second (and third and fourth) review of every order. Your CEO declares that *"we'll keep adding staff to Order Entry until every shipment goes out correctly."*

  Defensive? *Sure.* Good investment? *Probably not.* Wearing your "product champion" hat, you should be looking for ways to avoid the **cause** of this problem, not the symptom. Perhaps you need preconfigured bundles that meet actual customer needs. Or clearer channel discount policies. Or fewer price list updates. Maybe it's time to drop a few slow-moving products entirely. I'd bet that both Sales and Order Admin know precisely why customers are unable to ask for the right combination of stuff, and are waiting to tell you.

- **Copying everyone in Marketing (or Sales) on everything.** As departmental staff expands, several people may be working on related projects or talking with the same customers. Resellers get confused about where in Sales or Marketing to call. Some managers decide the best solution is to send ever-more-detailed status reports to increasingly wider audiences: *"We need daily project reports from each of you to the rest of the department. And all inquiries to our info@mystartup.com alias should be copied to the entire Sales/Marketing team."* Instantly, your inbox (and outbox) are crammed full of CYA messages. The hours each day you spend skimming each others' status reports increase frustration and resentment, but not productivity or teamwork. Better solutions would start with a sensible division of labor, clear project ownership, and a single person who can sort incoming inquiries. As your company grows, a simple "who does what" chart works wonders.

- **Tightly Managing Office Supplies.** If you're paying knowledge workers to be creative, they need reasonable access to PostIt™ notes and dry-erase markers. Even if a few pens wander home from the office. Enough said.

What's the common theme? Misdirected energy and misdiagnosed causes. Defensive organizations tend to address symptoms, substituting brute force scrutiny for clear thinking. This is less risky than asking whether a process actually benefits customers.

Before putting a cumbersome process in place, someone needs to consider its value. Typically, that falls to a startup's product champion – whether you're officially in that role or not. This may be a difficult part to play, even an unwelcome one, but will earn you the immediate respect of your co-workers.

YES, BUT...

Of course, not all defensive processes are bad. Please don't skip these:

- **Trademark searches.** If you're not an attorney, run new product names past someone who is. Urgency and layman's logic are poor second choices.
- **Quality Assurance.** QA is where you find out if your product actually works, and is ready to ship. Perennially underappreciated, QA engineers are the ones to catch everyone else's fuzzy thinking. Take them to lunch. Make them feel loved.
- **Clear Revenue Recognition Policies.** With Sarbanes-Oxley, you'll want to keep your CFO out of jail. More immediately, you'll also avoid dozens of angry discussions at quarter-end about which deals earn commission and which don't. Help your Sales team focus on real revenue. Avoid surprises.

Product champions are typically the first ones called to define new processes, or best asked to design them. We're also in the best position to spot procedures that inhibit progress or sap creative energy. The next time you trip over one of these clunkers, look for some alternate ways to reach the same goal. Or abandon it -- *what would happen if we didn't write one of our weekly reports?*

Consider if the procedure you're inventing answers a real need, or papers over a minor symptom.

SOUND BYTE

Processes are not naturally good or bad. It's all about results, effectiveness and motivating the right behaviors. Especially at a startup, initiative and insight need breathing room as well as rigor.

Growing Back into Management

JULY 2004

There's a funny paradox about joining a tiny company and helping it grow. If part of its attractiveness is an intimacy and lack of management overhead, success creates its own challenges.

Very small companies can operate on informal communications: all ten employees know what each other are doing. The entire staff can grab lunch together, and all-hands meetings easily fit into the conference room. News is shared over the cube wall. Job descriptions and titles are afterthoughts. Decisions are made in the aisle.

For those of us who've left big companies, part of the start-up fun is in getting our hands dirty again with actual work: customer requirements, product positioning, competitive analysis, business models, crafting the first PowerPoint, sketching out pricing strategies. *The work itself.* Mix the right products and markets together (with a boatload of luck), and you may be able to touch off explosive growth in customers and revenue. And staff.

THE WONDER YEARS

Suddenly, the entire team no longer fits around the conference table. New hires don't know all of the old-timers, and need to be told about the company's founding. Your newest sales rep lives across the country, and wonders who to call for things. Engineering (finally) asks for a formal mechanism to rank enhancement requests. Folks demand an employee phone list and an email alias for each department. Titles and job descriptions appear. The CEO talks about having an HR department and new hire orientation. *Boom!* Your infant start-up has become an awkward adolescent.

The organization is in desperate need of classic management: the team-building, weekly status reports, communications meetings, collective goal-setting, crisp role definition, org-chart-with-formal-titles kind of interpersonal leadership. Although managers don't do direct hands-on work, you need those indispensable folks to coordinate teams, define goals, wrestle for resources, negotiate charters, motivate, communicate, network, empower, decide. Your tiny start-up has grown enough to need... *well...* management.

One rule of thumb is that organizations have to add a new layer of management each time they triple their total staff. A company of 10 needs a CEO. A company of 30 also needs VPs. At 90, expect to see Directors as well as VPs.

AYE, THERE'S THE RUB

Which brings us back to the original paradox. You may have carefully honed your organizational skills and management tools at BigCorp, but you've used that success to buy a return trip to Smallville. For me, start-ups are about more than pure financial upside: they include the joy of working tough issues directly. Authoring the solution, not just reviewing it. That's hard to maintain when hiring the next four staffers, and as the calendar fills up with monthly project reviews.

Yet that's what success looks like. It's what we want. Taking revenue from $3M to $30M and staff from 12 to 100 is on every page of the business plan. Running out of available cubicles is cause for celebration. Our 100th customer. *Bigger is better.*

And thus the push back up into management. How to reconcile organizational needs with a desire to keep one hand in the work?

Here are a variety of alternatives, starting with the least appetizing:

- **Only join failures.** While this may keep you out of the management conundrum, it has some unpleasant side effects including unemployment. And you may still be fooled by the occasional diamond in the rough.

- **Keep your company from growing.** Usually even worse than a natural failure, since this means holding back the rest of your team. (*One exception is a professional services firm where the team plans to stay small, such as a specialty law practice.*)

- **Partner, outsource.** You may be able to license key technologies, hire marketing agencies, or send work outside. All of this needs to be coordinated and managed, however, and may cost more than hiring the team you need. Besides, if these outside folks were good, they'd be in their own start-ups.

- **Quit for something smaller.** If you're truly allergic to multiple management tiers, trade down when you have to. You'll need to warn your co-founders up front, though, and plan a very graceful transition. Suddenly leaving your company will leave you with a big smudge on your reputation.

- **Keep the organization flat.** This works temporarily, with peer roles defined ever more narrowly. When each VP has 15 direct reports, though, some layering will have to happen.

- **Hire your boss.** If you want to keep your hands dirty with the real work, find someone else to attend meetings and make decisions for you. Pick a person that you can actually work for, however, since bosses tend to take charge. (*And upside-down organizations are even more dysfunctional than flat ones.*)

- **Suck it up.** What's good for the company is good for you, and they need you in management now. Step up and stop whining about self-actualization. This is what you wanted to happen, on your way to a pricey exit strategy.

These range from the stark to the silly. In a real organization, change happens gradually and with plenty of time to plan. In large organizations, the same process happens at the departmental or divisional level, with similar challenges.

Or...

One practical solution is to carve out a few bits of "real" work to keep while taking on more of the formal management. These might be as executive sponsor for a major customer (*thus touching real product issues*), designing some reporting processes for Tech Support (*and seeing what this week's hot issues are*) or owning a key OEM relationship (*to mediate between direct and indirect deals*). Setting aside 10% of the week for hands-on customer contact may take the edge off of full-time management.

SOUND BYTE

Companies of every size need some management. The right mix for a small company – and its intentionally down-scaled execs – may be a dash of gritty reality alongside more traditional command and control.

Who's Calling Customer Support?

OCTOBER 2007

At most software companies, incoming calls to Tech Support don't match up against customer databases. We've worked on this with several clients to identify causes and jointly design solutions. It provides a great case study for how product managers should think: segmenting issues and balancing competing interests as the "CEOs of their products."

Setting up this scenario, imagine that your software company sells to thousands of large and small corporate customers. Customer Support is taking lots of calls from people that are not in the customer database. Some callers want technical help, others are asking for product upgrades or rebates. Your support manager is complaining about unhappy users and struggling to determine how to handle each caller.

As a product manager, your first reaction should be to tear this into a few different pieces – each of which may need its own solution. You might group these, for instance, into:

- Legitimate paying customers that we don't have contact information for
- Customers with expired support contracts
- Non-paying users, including pirates and users of expired trial software

The best product managers work in an agile manner: looking for quick partial solutions that deliver immediate business value while also driving long-term strategic items. Putting on our agile hats, let's consider each segment for possible improvement.

IDENTIFYING AND TRACKING REAL CUSTOMERS

It's hard to get customer information from sales channels, and even harder to get end users to register for support. In the corporate space, product managers have a grab bag of partial solutions to legitimately capture customer support information.

- **Improved internal data handling and housekeeping**. Your shipping and fulfillment groups may know where products are going: look for feedback from your ops processes.

- **Sales incentives**. If you have a direct sales force, *someone* knows each customer. Consider a "no contact info, no commission" policy enforced through your sales automation system. Then reduce the griping by paying commissions to your reps for service renewals. (For channel sales, think about optional co-marketing funds to align incentives.)

- **Nagware**. End users who fill in pop-up requests for registration could get extended support or faster responses. (Stop pestering them when they refuse three times.)

- Require users to **register online** with a company email before they can get support. At a minimum, you can verify that email address when delivering login information. And most amateur software pirates are reluctant to involve their companies in petty software theft.

- **Offer useful information to registered users**. Done right, how-to newsletters can build brand loyalty while simultaneously reducing support calls. Avoid hard-sell marketing in these vehicles.

"BUT I'M SURE THAT MY SUPPORT CONTRACT WAS RENEWED"

Our second group of callers insists that their support contracts are still current. *"The renewal check is in the mail"* or *"your paper-work processes must be running slow"*. Customer Support needs help with clear policies, signed off by your CFO, so that they know what to do. Product Managers win applause with common-sense answers like:

- **Offer a per-incident charge**. Choose an appropriate price (say $75 per incident or $90 per hour via credit card), with the first charge credited against support renewal. This generates revenue, encourages renewals, and undercuts the myth that support should be free.

- **Have a "hot accounts" list**. Your Sales VP should provide a monthly list of the top 10 prospects and problem accounts. If someone calls Support from these companies, route it to your top analyst and ignore any formalities. I've seen great support engineers pull accounts out of the fire and back into the revenue column.

- **15 days' grace**. If the contract expired on October 20th and a call comes in October 28th, just help the customer.

Tech Support is generally understaffed and under-appreciated. They will join your fan club if you can create good, clear policies.

THAR BE PIRATES

And finally, some folks have the nerve to call you for support after stealing your software. They are willing to spend a lot of *their* time to get free service and software from you. Don't waste your energy trying to get revenue from pirates, especially if it inconveniences your legitimate customers.

Think like a CEO, then, about the net effect on your business of implementing license keys or digital rights management (DRM). There are great vendors with proven solutions in this space (we've worked with Aladdin and Macrovision, or check out SIIA) with solutions based on installation codes, hardware tokens, system fingerprinting, and other ways of tracking legal software deployments. Done correctly, you'll minimize customer inconvenience, and may get substantial benefits, such as a superdistribution and segment-specific bundles of features. Done poorly, you'll create confusion and put your job at risk. (*Remember Sony BMG's DRM fiasco?*)

 SOUND BYTE

Support and licensing issues are complex. Product Managers need to think broadly, balance the support of non-customers against complexity for paying customers, and keep a bias towards customer satisfaction. Even, at times, among the pirates.

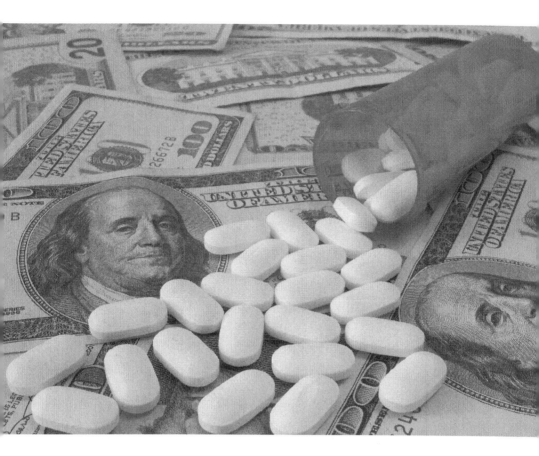

Hallucinogenic Funding

I n the pre-boom venture model, companies got enough funding in their early rounds to build preliminary products and test-market them to selected customers. Once they had found some market validation, VCs followed with larger funding *tranches* to fuel an expansion of sales and marketing. This encouraged early exploration and later (timely) spending. In the bubble, this was reversed: great concepts were fully funded up-front, with some interesting side effects. Here are some thoughts on how excessive early funding can warp a start-up's perception.

AREN'T WE PAST OVERFUNDING?

Although huge VC injections are out of fashion, I still see overfunding in selected (hot) segments. For example... the next generation of wireless infrastructure is just coming to market, and there are some interesting innovations. One good thought is to marry wireless Access Points (APs) and the wired switches that support them, adding software that coordinates all of the pieces for better security and coverage. *Oops. Nothing spreads faster than a good idea.* There may be more than 50 companies about to deliver "AP/switch" solutions including **AirFlow**, **AirGo**, **Airespace**, **Aruba**, **Chantry**, **Legra**, **Trapeze** and **Vivato** – each a start-up with a unique approach to the problem.

Similarly, I'd love a truly effective anti-spam product to wrestle the hundreds of junk items coming to me each day, and corporate email managers are even more anxious for solutions. I've tried **SpamAssassin, SpamNet**, and am now using **Qurb**. A good market opportunity is easy to overpopulate, however. At last count, more than 80 firms were crowding into this niche.

In most new markets, a few start-ups receive massive early funding doses. They have the chance to inhale a lot of Sand Hill pixie dust. *(Full disclosure: I'm just as guilty. There's none so righteous as a recovering VC addict. I try to attend meetings when I'm not pitching new business plans...)* With such potent finances in the organizational bloodstream, it's easy to believe in your start-up's invulnerability.

A FIVE MIS-STEP PROGRAM

So you've joined the newest high-concept start-up. Investors are excited, with some shoving to get into a massive "A" round. (Everyone breathes in deeply.) How does this excessive funding affect your judgment?

1. **"We're Right."** It's easy to believe that raising $50M or $100M proves that customers will buy your proposition. A big war chest certainly gives you time to pursue your vision. The biggest advantage of a start-up, however, is the ability to get rapid product feedback and swerve with the market. Deep pockets let you ignore critical inputs, and continue spending on "market education."

   Hank Chesbrough's research on spin-offs and start-ups shows that small companies succeed precisely because they are forced to serve real needs. Short on cash, they find actual customers with tangible problems -- and re-arrange their product visions to fit the real world. A daily dose of financial terror clears the mind.

2. **"We make a product, not just a feature."** Tiny companies have the luxury of considering different business models. For instance, some choose an OEM strategy, embedding their value-added software into other products for a small royalty. (**Meetinghouse Communications** does this well for low-end Wi-Fi authentication.) Potential competitors can be turned into customers.

   You're now part of an important, well-funded company, however. Important companies sell products to end customers. To do so, you'll need to deliver something that is highly differentiated. Most likely, you'll also have to match the feature set of whatever last-generation product you hope to replace – and which has evolved though a dozen releases. Your engineers started with a handful of innovative algorithms, but they inherited a truckload of generic features that you need to displace incumbent vendors.

3. **"This is a $1B market."** If you've taken $75M from investors, they will want $750M back later. This usually forces you to pursue a very large market with premium-priced products. Selling a few thousand copies of software at $1000 each won't impress your Board of Directors. In fact, you probably predicted a billion-dollar market in order to raise this money… and are not eager to downsize your forecasts. *(Hint: very few $1B markets exist, and yours is not the first team to spot this one.)* Now

you're forced into overly aggressive goals and assumptions, which create organizational pressure to ignore what you hear from the market. Staffing plans are built against very optimistic targets. Leading to...

4. **"We need to get big fast."** To dominate a $1B market, you need to sell $20M in the first year. This calls for six or eight fully staffed regional sales teams. Even though your product isn't ready to sell, you'll equip each team with PowerPoints, data sheets, price lists, logo pens, ROI models, and other bits of science fiction. After all, you've identified a compelling need and expect to close dozens of customers within 60 days of product availability. *As if.* Throw in an inevitable schedule slip or two, and Sales will insist that...

5. **"PR and Marketing can accelerate customer adoption."** Hardly. Most corporate marketplaces develop slowly. *(Dust off your unread copy of "Crossing the Chasm." It's still valid.)* IT buyers are risk-averse. Each will want reference accounts, extended evaluation periods, and budget approval time. Many customers have incumbent vendors with political support. Regardless, your sales force will demand qualified leads. Here's your chance to spend some of that idle cash on a massive PR blitz and multi-city road show - well in advance of final product. If the press loves your story, then perhaps Gartner and Forrester will be unwilling to point out the obvious.

We've all seen companies expand too fast, too soon, and overshoot the market. Revving the Sales & Marketing machine in advance of customer demand is tempting, and often asked for. **It's like burning down your house to keep warm, however**. After a wild night of marshmallows, cognac and cigars, you may need to find a new place to live.

The preemptive solution calls for humility and self-control: don't accept so much money. In practice, this is very hard to do - as demonstrated by generations of dieters and AA members.

After the fact, you should struggle to conserve your massive war chest for a well-timed expansion: keeping your powder dry instead of inhaling it. After some thoughtful wandering and market exploration, you'll be able to execute aggressively. *(Still, it's hard to resist when funding makes you feel so smart and so successful.)*

SOUND BYTE

Outside capital is a stimulant. Taking too much too early can blinker your judgment, make you feel omnipotent, and encourage risky behaviors. Most dangerous of all, it can help you ignore the market. Moderation in all things.

The Almost-New-New Things

Agile and Software-as-a-Service

Software-as-a-Service (SaaS) seems to be freshly discovered every few years, often as selected companies have IPOs or major financial events. In its current form, though, it's been underway for at least a decade. I was at a start-up called iPass in the middle '90s that provided pure transaction-priced Internet connection services (with software tossed in for free) and at Slam Dunk Networks to build a SaaS infrastructure for application message delivery. Regardless, the uptake on SaaS is huge and it presents some unique product management challenges. Several early SaaS-related columns are collected here.

In the same way, Agile has been emerging for a while, and is now (in 2008) just hitting the mainstream. Non-engineering executives are hearing about it for the first time, seven years after The Agile Manifesto was posted. The next big step for Agile is moving beyond the confines of Engineering organizations, into company-wide operations. With Agile product managers acting as simultaneous translators for Marketing, Sales, Finance and Support, we're seeing the first indications that Agile can deliver tangible, financially relevant results that customers and shareholders care about.

For me, "Agile" has been closely tied to "start-up" as Agile product folks drift away from very large (slow, bureaucratic, stifling) companies into a series of fresh adventures. There's some real hope, though, that huge organizations can get lighter on their feet. As Luke Hohmann says, "*Agile isn't something you do. Agile is something you are.*" Here's hoping you find your own brand of Agile.

The Accidental Agilist

W e've been hearing lately about product managers who come back from customer visits or vacations to discover that their engineering teams have *gone agile* without telling them. After which, the PMs scramble to figure out how their roles and deliverables are different under a new development model. They are either shut out of their organizations or abdicating a critical part of the product management mission.

I continue to see that Agile delivers more and better software; that product managers are an irreplaceable part of that improvement; and the PM function needs to be a champion of business improvements. All of which requires PMs to be intimately involved in the daily activities of their development teams, helping them be more successful.

WHERE IS THE PUSH FOR AGILE COMING FROM?

Software development works better under Agile - *and almost everything is software under the covers.* Software arrives faster, with higher quality, and with fewer huge strategic gaffes than waterfall models. That translates directly into measurable savings in cost and time, higher predictability, and sometimes improved revenue. The chance to boost development throughput by 30-40%

energizes CFOs and CIOs and CEOs, not just VPs of Engineering. This is no longer a "pick your poison" or religious discussion.

These are bold claims, so third party validation is important. Consider VeriSign, where the Managed Security Services team used Agile to largely replace traditional Marketing Requirements with roadmaps and backlogs, shaving an estimated 3 months from their development cycle. Or Israel Gat from BMC Software, who subjected his Agile process to intense public scrutiny, and demonstrated remarkable levels of quality and time-to-market for new releases. Key Bank and Capital One are some of the financial institutions sharing their successes with Agile, and our own work with Emerson Process Technology successfully applied Agile to development of extremely complex embedded systems.

*(If your PM team **isn't** considering and debating a shift to Agile, it will happen without your input. You could be the spouse who comes home from work, surprised to find that your key no longer opens the door to the house.)*

Directors and VPs of product management represent all constituents in this opportunity. They speak for the customer, buffer Engineering from excessive meddling, and own revenue-based product planning. As arbiters of trade-offs and balanced release maps, PMs are often best situated to advocate for changes in development methodology. Promoting *better-faster-smarter-cheaper* is central to the PM role.

Engineering teams want to do their best, and are filled with smart, well-informed, tightly networked folks. You're either helping them invent the future or reading about the results.

IS AGILE PM *REALLY* DIFFERENT?

From 100,000 feet, all product management, agile or traditional, looks the same. We size markets, understand customers, write requirements, solicit and interpret customer feedback, and work like mad to position products for Sales & Marketing. Just like getting from San Francisco to Boston is the same regardless of how you travel.

Even at 30,000 feet, though, you know the difference between flying and driving. Each may have indifferent food, movies for passengers, and ways to buy more expensive seats - but one gets you to Boston in 5 hours rather than 5 days.

Agile really is different from waterfall. Every day, almost every deliverable. You talk with Engineering differently, and (eventually) think about your products in a new way. Consider:

- **Customer Input.** Your waterfall model was to gather input, *then* write requirements, *then* hope for good outcomes next year. Under Agile, customer input is actively solicited throughout the development cycle: reviewing wire frames, early features and usability. We've found that traditional PMs struggle under their old mental model of striving to "deliver it perfectly" before showing something to customers instead of "collaboratively shaping the final result".

- **Development Team Collaboration.** To take advantage of all of this powerful customer input, Agile PMs meet with their development teams much more frequently than traditional PMs. The result is a much richer calibration of what the actual product needs to be successful in the marketplace.

- **Backlogs.** Your backlog is a dynamic, near-real-time set of deliverables for both Engineering and Product Management that you're constantly reviewing to reflect internal conditions and external opportunities. A key member of the team becomes sick? Change the backlog to reflect capacity. A deal comes along that you want to close but requires just a few more features? Reshuffle the backlog and then ship the software, secure in your knowledge that good Agile teams create "release ready" software *every* iteration.

- **User stories.** Back in the days of pocket protectors, PMs wrote complete (and lengthy) MRDs/PRDs intended to tell Engineering precisely what to build. These were immediately out of date, and failed to anticipate the many trade-offs in a year-plus development cycle, so we patched and updated them along with one-off priority decisions.

  Most Agile approaches create **more** documentation – not less – but timed to when the team needs it. Agilists prefer the consistent expression of user stories, which can be flexibly managed and developers easily understand. You may sketch out fifteen user stories and user experience guidelines, but initially complete only the first two stories in detail. The rest go onto your backlog. You will be elaborating user stories throughout the release cycle - just ahead of demand, when your customer knowledge is most complete.

- **Fewer unused features.** Items further down in your backlog might not get built. That's a good indicator that they weren't really needed, versus the "do it all now" PRD model.

- **Credible, fact-based status reports.** As your team gains some experience with Agile, they get better at estimation and judging their progress. More importantly, the focus on working software at the end of every iteration makes your traditional approach to assessing progress not only meaningless, but dangerous. You'll never again ask "Is this feature 80% complete?" and instead learn to work in "whole and complete" deliverables. Engineering will love seeing how this boosts credibility with Sales and Marketing.

Your initial PM reaction may be "*can I continue to do PM the way I've always done it, even though my engineering team is trying to be agile?*" You're driving, not flying, though until you rephrase this as "*how do I harness Engineering's added power?*"

YOU *WILL* NEED MORE HELP

Under Agile, there's a lot more work for an Agile PM to do. Our most successful clients are forming product teams of (for instance) product managers, program managers plus business analyst/requirements experts. Teams provide the extra attention and bandwidth – the Agile PM magic – that Engineering needs to deliver measurable productivity improvements.

Directors and VPs of product management need to address this head-on. Part of the cost of Agile is more PM talent. Practice saying this in front of your mirror: "*Nothing is free. In order to get the best out of Engineering, we'll need a few more PM resources, plus Agile training for the entire Engineering-Product team.*" Shifting a little of Engineering's savings into PM is more than reasonable.

SOUND BYTE

If Agile hasn't come to your software team, it will soon. The business benefits are irresistible. Product Management should be pushing for adoption and helping plan the transition, not waiting to be Accidental Agilists.

A Planetary View of Agile Product Management

NOVEMBER 2007

We at Enthiosys are often asked how the shift to Agile changes product management. We normally see PM at the center of everything, so it's natural to think about other functional organizations as planets in product-centric orbits - and what happens when we move to Agile.

Product management is involved with most internal groups, but **not equally** and not all at the same time. PMs need to exert enough gravitational pull to keep each organization in its correct orbit, and still save some energy for customers. So let's give our planetary analogy a spin.

STARTING WITH ENGINEERING . . .

In the traditional waterfall model, a typical project is scheduled for 9 months, but inevitably takes a year to complete. So we'll assign classic software development groups to **Earth** in our product solar system, with a 365 day cycle. A starting place that's warm, comfortable, and not surprisingly lines up with annual budgeting. Product Managers have some "pull" in the development process, but at a distance: we send out MRDs and PRDs to shed light on customer requirements, knowing that a lot is filtered out by the R&D atmosphere.

The move to Agile brings Engineering much closer: think about **Mercury** in its 88 day orbit. With sprints every two to four weeks and quarterly releases, we've seen a dramatic acceleration of the development process. PM is now a daily partner in every aspect of product creation, exerting much more pull to keep Engineering on course. Product managers now have a lot more to do - iteration planning and review meetings, backlog rankings, retrospectives - to keep things spinning. User stories and requirements arrive more often, in smaller chunks, as the team needs. So the Agile planet is faster, hotter, more nimble, as long as a good product manager is providing a tight focus.

OTHER IMPORTANT ORGANIZATIONS

A company's biggest groups are Sales and Marketing. Regardless of your development process, they are far away from the details of product creation. The obvious choices are **Jupiter** and **Saturn**: large, distant, with massive budgets and extremely long planning cycles. Editorial calendars, trade shows and branding campaigns may be booked 1-2 years ahead, and enterprise selling cycles can be glacial. *(Let's match Marketing to Saturn, since rings attract creative types, and Sales to Jupiter, the gas giant.)*

Product folks need to remember that messages to distant planets take a long time, even at Internet speeds, and the payload has to be small. Therefore, we need to ***repeatedly*** send **short, simplified messages** to Sales and Marketing rather than detailed, time-sensitive feature lists. Hefty documents often arrive late and become space debris.

Occasionally, individual sales reps act like **Halley's Comet**, flying by with a hot opportunity. They spend most of their time with distant customers, but sometimes need your help closing a complex deal. Comets move fast, so you'll need to make a quick judgment whether this opportunity is a good fit for your product: Agile provides an opportunity to adjust your backlog and release plans. In any case, you may not see this particular rep for another 75 years.

Some other important functions are in danger of being treated like **Pluto**: considered frozen wastelands and downgraded to sub-planet stature. This might include Tech Support or Manufacturing or even QA. If you see this, remember that PMs can make a big difference by shining a light on their accomplishments and including them in appropriate meetings. A little light and warmth from PM can change the company climate.

Finally, Finance and Legal: a pair of **asteroids** that need to be mapped and managed to avoid a surprise impact. Keep them in the loop. You may discover something valuable beneath their battered, pock-marked exteriors.

PM has the challenge of keeping different organizations in their respective orbits and preventing collisions. Cycle times vary dramatically. Since cross-functional communications can be slow, send out capsule updates early and often.

SOUND BYTE

Product Managers exert the most influence over development, and Agile makes this even stronger. We need to stay connected with other groups, pulling each along the path to success. Done right, we drive alignment behind great products.

Burning Through Product Managers

SEPTEMBER 2007

A gile software development methods are rapidly being adopted by companies across a wide variety of industries and company sizes because it's a better way to build software. At several Enthiosys clients, however, we're seeing product managers ("PMs") struggle as the product management role becomes more intensely collaborative within an agile development process.

WHY ARE PM'S STRUGGLING?

Traditionally, PMs used to send bulky product requirements to engineering - then wait 9+ months for alpha versions and early customer feedback. This left plenty of time for the "outbound" part of product management: customer meetings, competitive analysis, roadmaps, pricing, drafting of feature matrices and data sheet copy, and the prep work that parallels long development cycles.

In a typical agile model, PMs replace this document-centric approach with rapid collaboration. This creates an additional 10+ hours of work per week elaborating and clarifying requirements; rapidly reviewing user interfaces and customer-facing product elements; quickly removing development roadblocks; and broadly supporting the team. These additional hours are on top of the half day or more allocated to sprint planning and retrospective meetings every 2-3 weeks.

For the team as a whole, this is great news: injecting customer awareness in every phase of development through intensive PM involvement is one of the reasons agile delivers better software faster. Product managers, though, may struggle under the added load.

WHAT ARE THE SYMPTOMS?

By nature and role, PMs take on a wide range of nebulous and under-defined tasks that don't have other owners. This makes it hard to define exactly what gets postponed if agile PMs hit overload.

When we hear an engineering team complaining that their product manager no longer spends enough time in sprint planning, review, or retrospective meetings, we suspect that PM is allowing outside responsibilities (meeting with customers, training sales teams, performing competitive market research) take priority over inside collaborations. Alternatively, when clients tell us that product are no longer selling well because a product manager is unaware of changing market conditions, we can spot a product manager spending too much time with engineering.

And if nothing is getting done, product management burn-out is as likely as organizational grid-lock.

PMs not prepared for agile's additional overhead may fail to recognize how overextended they are. They won't complain - preferring to be sleepless rather than be labeled as "whiners." The shift to agile has implications for PM staffing, training and organization.

If you are managing teams of PMs, you need to be especially alert for exhaustion.

SO WHAT SHOULD WE DO?

Identifying problems is always a good first step toward solutions. As product management executives, we (you) should be:

- **Reviewing PM-to-Product Team ratios.** I've personally managed 7 products concurrently using waterfall methods. For agile, though, this won't work. Consider just the stand-up and sprint planning meetings for each product, and you'll see a natural limit of 1 to 2 products per PM. If you're on the path to agile, plan some time for organizational design.

- **Getting PMs trained in agile.** They will be twice as productive in half the time with some good agile PM training and mentoring. You need to schedule this for them as most PMs won't allow themselves time to learn about the next wave.

- **Revisiting agile meeting schedules.** Newly agile teams often create redundant meetings, so PMs should be encouraged to cancel or opt out of duplicate meetings. Developers can pick small tasks off the backlog themselves; weekly bug priority meetings can be short (if development pre-ranks all bugs and PMs resolve disagreements).

- **Consider Creating Product Duos or Trios.** We see the most productive agile companies pairing a product manager with a program manager, splitting decision-making from task management. A business requirements analyst who can elaborate backlog items created by product managers makes this even more effective, creating a highly productive trio.

- **Watching for burn-out.** Great PMs don't complain and may not recognize how overextended they are. As product executives, we need to protect and nourish our PMs the same way they protect and nourish their products.

SOUND BYTE

Agile development drives the need for more intensive product management involvement in the day to day activities so while the engineering may celebrate a great burn down chart, it may be burning up your product managers. To avoid PM burn-out make sure your product team is staffed, trained and appreciated for taking on this bigger role.

Grocers and Chefs:
Software Service Models

MAY 2007

'\
've talked with many companies considering a shift from traditional licensing models to hosted software-as-a-service (SaaS).
It's important to recognize the radical changes such a move
may force within your entire company. Let's serve up a metaphor
for the mental and organizational adjustments needed to move
from a "product" model to a service business.

FIRST, YOU'RE A GROCER

Traditionally, most enterprise software has been sold under a
licensing model: your sales team patiently harasses customers
until they agree to take your software. You then send a CD along
with an invoice, completing the transaction. The customer is
responsible for implementation, integration, network security, and
extracting some value out of your expertly crafted bits.

To kick off our metaphor, **licensed software vendors are grocers**. Grocers sell poultry and onions and carrots, but it's not their
job to decide if the home-made chicken soup needs more salt.

Likewise, as a licensed software vendor, you've left it up to IT
departments at your enterprise customers to choose the right applications, combine them correctly, decide when solutions are ready,
and ultimately serve end users with what they need. You deliver
an assortment of software bits, get a signature on the purchase

order, and tip your hat on the way out. *Off to find another enterprise that needs your product set!*

If, for instance, your company sells resumé-scanning software to corporate HR departments, you expect your customers to buy server hardware, assign user passwords, take calls from confused end users, monitor disk space, and handle complaints from HR managers who don't like your application.

Given the buzz around software-as-a-service, though, your company's new strategic direction is to transform itself into a hosted service: HR managers everywhere will point *their* browsers to *your* server and run your resumé-scanning application over the Internet. You'll charge each a monthly user fee.

NOW YOU'RE A CHEF!

In a restaurant, the chef must cook and deliver complete meals for each guest. He's responsible for the entire dining experience: no excuses about ingredients, faulty ovens, or short-staffed kitchens. Food is available on demand – any time the door is open, customers can come in for a hot meal.

Congratulations! By hosting an application centrally, you've put on a chef's apron. Your company now **directly** serves each individual HR manager, and is responsible for their success. You've taken on the entire range of operational and support functions needed to serve up working applications. Presentation counts: every login is an opportunity to impress users – or fail to deliver.

SO WHAT WILL YOU NEED?

You'll have at least four new sets of challenges/opportunities in the shift from licensed software to software-as-a-service:

- **Shared Infrastructure.** Also called multi-tenancy, this means that your application must serve many users transparently, giving each a personal experience and protecting one client's data from the next. Converting an existing free-standing application to multi-tenancy can be a huge challenge, so don't attempt this without a SaaS-experienced software architect. There are also infrastructure players with multi-tenant-enabled platforms -- see for instance AppExchange, Cordys and Ekartha.

    In food terms, this is the transition from throwing a dinner party for twenty *[one menu, one serving time, invited guests]* to a ten-table restaurant *[choice of food, staggered arrival times, strangers to please]*. Corporate IT has traditionally served up the "application of the day" while SaaS providers have to satisfy broader tastes.

- **Incremental Sales Cycles.** Enterprise buyers of service-model software tend to start with a few users, and slowly expand their subscriptions. This is one of the big selling points of SaaS: **customers can start small, without making huge financial commitments.** Early subscribers get to sample the service before recommending it to their co-workers... which translates directly into slower revenue ramps.

    Licensed software companies, though, are used to big ticket sales with up-front revenue, long before the customer gets any use out of the product. Their marketing strategy and sales commissions don't translate well in the new on-demand world, and need to be overhauled. Think of customers who can buy (and taste!) the appetizers before committing to a full meal. Every online interaction is your chance for good reviews – or unappetizing comments to prospects.

- **Itemized Billing.** Corporate IT may allocate application costs to departments, but it rarely needs to track and account for individual user activity. IT budgets are allocated for bulk user advantage.

  Service-based models must (by definition) be able to track each user's activity, then bill and invoice correctly. Many on-demand services fall back on monthly "*all you can eat*" subscriptions because they can't manage any usage-based accounting. They are missing the chance to fine-tune their value propositions and revenue models, unknowingly leaving money on the table. Think hard about your service pricing strategy and build the audit trail to support it. "**Separate checks, please!**"

- **Real Usage Information.** Enterprise product managers have a devil of a time finding out what features their end users actually use. We field endless surveys, host round tables, and beg to look over customers' shoulders. Results are incomplete, biased, anecdotal.

  In this new world, though, service-model product folks suddenly have a new weapon – the activity logs in their hosted systems. SaaS vendors can directly ask and answer interesting questions about user preferences by looking at their customers' online transactions. B2C players like Google and Amazon have always known this, but enterprise folks are still catching up. *(I surveyed service PMs and found that 75% were not reading their activity logs.)* Make sure you're using the new information that's served up for you.

And so on. It's clear that moving to a service model is much more than just hosting a copy of your existing software. **You must be willing to supplement your organization with fresh skills and new kinds of talent.** Not all software companies have the self-awareness to recognize what's missing, or the daring to redesign their organizations as service vendors.

It's the same for your friend whose *crème brûlée* is to die for. Not obvious that she should rent a building, hire a staff, and start a restaurant.

SOUND BYTE

Discussions about shifting to a service model are inevitable. Now's the time to consider what new ingredients your company will need to serve up tasty on-demand offerings, and how service-ready your team is. Open up your requirements cookbook, dust off a set of performance measuring spoons, and start an on-demand application shopping list.

So Your Product
Wants to Be a Service...

OCTOBER 2002

S ometimes we take a fresh look at a product, with the thought of turning it into a service. This is *especially* attractive if sales of our product-as-a-product are less than planned. Here's a short exploration of the opportunities and pitfalls in moving from a product model to a service model.

First, we'll step through some successful service models including application hosting, transaction-based, and subscriptions. Then, sketch an example to highlight some of the advantages and challenges of services versus classic product sales.

APPLICATION HOSTING

Also known as the ASP (Application Service Provider) model, application hosting runs customer applications from an external data center or Internet resource. Upshot.com does this for sales force automation; NetLedger offloads small business accounting and ERP; Instill manages supply chains for large foodservice operators.

Most ASPs fail, though. Competition is fierce and differentiation is rare. For example, thousands of email and web providers are fighting for the $6.00 I spend each month hosting mironov.com. (Remember Exodus and Corio?) Open source solutions and cheap hardware make generic hosted services a rush to the bottom.

TRANSACTION-BASED

Lots of services charge by the drink (or trade or trip or teleconference or session or mortgage quote). Usually, these companies are not really in the software business at all, but offer an explicit service. Schwab sells stock trades, even though they provide several slick client-server tools. iPass charges for worldwide broadband and dial-up access by the minute, after hiding some awesome software under the hood. Cellular services are the prime example of paying for "free hardware" one minute at a time.

You'll notice, though, that service providers have to keep marketing to you. Newsletters and special offers are designed to encourage transactions. If you forget about them, they may just cease to exist. They also consider software a cost item – necessary but not a direct source of revenue.

PAYING FOR FRESHNESS

Finally, some software is only useful because it is current. Imagine Norton AntiVirus running last January's infection profiles. Likewise, TurboTax will need a yearly forms upgrade as long as there are politicians in Washington. Smart marketers package subscriptions or updates for these rare beasts.

Most products can't get away with "freshness dating." Microsoft's recent "Software Assurance" plan moves Windows toward a subscription model – and has infuriated customers. Corporate CTOs believe that operating software is a product that they buy rather than rent. We'll see if Microsoft drives large segments of its frustrated buyers to LINUX desktops.

HOW ABOUT AN EXAMPLE?

Putting a little theory into action, imagine that you are the product champion for a hot new security verification tool. Your brainchild can inspect web-based .NET applications for the 20 most obvious security holes — vulnerabilities created by naïve developers using Microsoft's new app construction kit. Your sales team started selling this as a packaged product at $4000 per copy plus $1000 per year for updates (to cover the frequent discoveries of new .NET gaffes). Unfortunately, your quarterly revenue has not made the investors smile.

You could host this as a service and charge developers $200 per scan. With no upfront cash and no commitments from your target customers, who could possibly resist? Besides, every .NET story in InformationWeek highlights the need for your service.

Good news about this possible strategic shift:

- Very low entry prices can knock down sales barriers. Customers don't pay large up-front license fees, and can be coaxed to sample your service with free trial offers.
- Services are a renewable resource. Customers buy them fresh each time.
- Good services are habit-forming. (That's why we call them "users." Most services give you a month free and hope to get you hooked.)

Of course, these benefits have immediate costs:

- Suddenly, your revenue model has slowed down. **S-l-o-o-o-o-w-e-d**. A customer has to use your scanning service 20 times to reach the original license fee. It might take 6 (or 12 or 18) months for an average customer to ring up $4000.

- Customers can walk away as easily as they arrive. Your security checker had better be terrific to earn the loyalty of users, and be trivially easy to operate. Expect to answer a flood of naïve support questions.

- Occasional users of your service will get a real bargain, and heavy users will demand deep discounts (or force you to sell them the original $4000 product). To make your numbers, you will need a much larger base of infrequent users than with a packaged software model.

Hmmmm. Not clear that shifting from product to service is a win here. If you're having trouble finding enough .NET developers willing to buy a $4000 security testing packages, the problem may be bigger than service-versus-product.

 ## SOUND BYTE

Picking a service model for your product may not be obvious. You need to put on your end customer thinking cap, then map out the revenue stream to make sure you'll live long enough to succeed. Consider pricing tiers attractive to occasional as well as heavy users. Call me if you're not sure what to do next.

The "Null Service"

JUNE 2003

As customers get more interested in hosted services and ASPs, a lot of product teams are re-conceiving their packaged software as outsourced Internet offerings. The assumptions and infrastructure needed for **hosting** a service, however, are very different from traditional licensed software. Hosted corporate applications need an underlying architectural layer that is missing from internal apps -- but roughly consistent across ASP offerings. I've been calling this the "**null service**."

First some history. Years ago at Sybase, we had lots of discussions about the "null release." This was shorthand for the effort needed to put out a new version of a software product **independent** of the specific changes being made to it. Imagine a one-line fix to Sybase's enterprise middleware suite, which then had to be ported to 31 operating systems, run through QA, compatibility tested, documented, released, staged for customer upgrades and announced. This might represent 4 months work for 45 people, at a cost of $2M. The "null release" concept helped balance demands for ever-more-frequent release cycles against the fixed cost of production.

Moving forward a decade to the emergence of hosted services and ASPs, here's our related concept: the "null service." This is the technical infrastructure needed to run **any** online service for business – regardless of its specifics – if the service must be secured, hosted, billed for, and generally available to all of its users. Said another way, there is a common set of systems and procedures that most web-based applications should have.

How does pondering the "null service" help? Early in the planning cycle, it lets a marketing and development team cleave large projects in half – with one group focused on well-understood infrastructure while another concentrates on defining detailed service features. Part of the implementation work can begin right away, in parallel with market analysis.

HOW ABOUT AN EXAMPLE?

Imagine that your company is the leader in outplacement application software. The world's largest corporations license your solution to track successive waves of employee downsizing -- assuring HR executives that seniority rules have been followed, and that no Federal statutes have been violated. *(This is fictional, remember?)* Corporate customers run your software on their own systems, however, and pay you $500,000+ each for the privilege. You believe that a much larger market exists as an Internet service if you can lower the price and skinny down the features. By hosting a lightweight version of your application online, you can reach thousands of mid-sized companies that might need to cut staff some day.

True to form, your software designers want a precise map of service features before they start development. To create it, your marketing team needs extensive customer research to pick the few important features from among your hundreds of configuration options. This requirements-gathering cycle will take six months of customer interviews and design work before the first line of application code is written.

SHOULD WE WAIT FOR THE PERFECT MRD?

Don't wait! Now is a great time to begin laying the groundwork for your "null service." Regardless of which downsizing features you include, the solution will have to have:

- Hot stand-by systems for application and database fail-over
- Account information identifying each customer (and each user)
- Password issuance, plus a procedure for replacing lost passwords
- Security to keep each customer's staff cuts hidden from others
- A billing module to send invoices, enroll new customers, show usage-to-date, and cut off 60-day-past-due accounts
- An uptime commitment or Service Level Agreement (SLA), along with reports to measure actual uptime
- Operational procedures for validating software updates and staging them without customer downtime, plus a way to back them out if needed
- "Thank you for enrolling" emails with instructions and URLs for more help
- Self-help portal for current and prospective users
- Customer support processes (email or phone?) with committed response times
- 60-day reminders in advance of annual renewals

- Marketing e-newsletter with subscribe/unsubscribe mechanism
- Posted privacy policy for your e-newsletter
- ...

You get the idea. There is a lot of work queued up, and much of it could be started today. Decisions about how your application should calculate exit packages (or whatever) don't make any difference to uptime strategies, password management or newsletter opt-in policies.

Many of these underlying hosting technologies will be managed by an Operations team. This is a crack set of network and production engineering folks who keep your service running in the face of power outages, typhoons, locusts, sudden peaks in end user traffic, carrier bankruptcy, and email viruses. **An Operations group doesn't exist in your current "licensed software" model**, but will be critical to the success of any hosted service. Finding them may take a while.

A big part of the Operations puzzle is the design of people processes: detailed steps to do seemingly simple things. Who will take customer support calls and how quickly will we respond? What happens when a customer wants a partial refund half-way through a subscription period? How do we verify that a password re-issue request is legitimate?

AND THEN...

Ultimately, these two major pieces -- core functional development and Operations -- will have to come together. For instance, you may decide that each account will have several kinds of users (HR managers, outplacement specialists, and ex-employees), which forces some fiddling with login security to set permissions correctly. This then implies a procedure for customers to give out end user accounts, and so on. Having six extra months to design a foundation will speed your implementation and reduce last-minute panic.

Eventually, the "utility computing" initiatives from HP and IBM may meet application infrastructure dreams like Jamcracker and SalesForce's <u>sforce</u>. This could give us a complete hosted 'shell' for paid, production-quality Internet services -- like the e-commerce and logistics framework that Amazon provides for Target. For now, though, you should plan on architecting most of this in-house.

SOUND BYTE

While you're planning the details of your Internet service, you should also start mapping out the generic infrastructure that you'll inevitably need. Don't wait for perfect application clarity to get your operations design underway.

Getting into Customers' Heads

Much of product management is about trying to understand customers: what they want, what they say they want, and what they really need. Luke Hohmann, Enthiosys founder and CEO, has written a great book about this called Innovation Games®, which lays out some very powerful tools for qualitative research.

The following articles, though, came before my meeting up with Enthiosys. Each represents a different slice of the customer problem. They all reflect the need to think **like** your customer, rather than just **about** your customer.

More broadly, good product folks spent time pretending to be each of the people in their product's value chain: actual end users, buyers, sales reps, channel partners, competitors, beta testers, and the internal technical support team that must eventually explain how things actually work.

We accumulate beliefs about how the world should be – how prospects should evaluate our goods, what every end user knows before installing our products, how much mindshare we deserve with our resellers. But the world turns out to be wonderfully complex and unpredictable. When I venture out into the marketplace, I'm almost always surprised. And rarely disappointed.

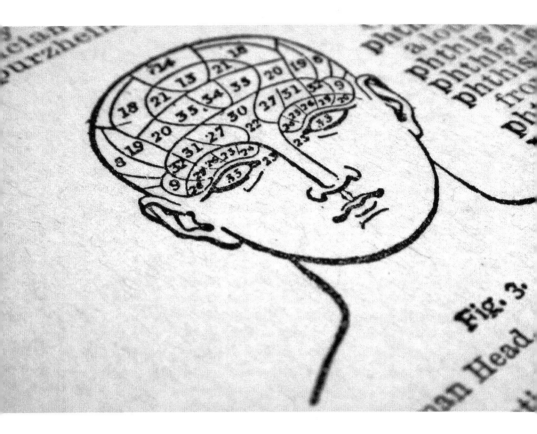

Fig. 3.

an Head.

Getting into Customers' Heads

AUGUST 2002

S ometimes, at the end of a heroic development effort, we find lukewarm prospects instead of purchase-order-waving customers. How can we get inside our prospects' heads early in the product cycle so that our "next new thing" meets their needs and desires?

Or, paraphrasing Freud's famous question about women, **"What do customers want**?"

This question generates a ton of frustration in both early-stage and later-stage companies. Marketing and Sales are frustrated by Engineering's inability to build products that do what customers want. Engineering repeatedly complains about "incomplete requirements." It often becomes an argument about what **we think** customers should want.

The most effective way to find out what early-stage customers want is to ask. *(Gasp!)* Individually. In detail. With our mouths shut.

Large consumer products companies have spent decades fine-tuning focus groups and lifestyle interviews to learn how we feel about shampoo or toothpaste. Similarly, established technology firms have an installed base of customers to survey. How does a start-up attack this problem, especially when it may not yet have a product built or any paying customers?

One successful approach is the "**customer use case**" – sometimes called a deployment scenario. It describes in exquisite detail how one customer might take advantage of our new thing. In my experience, it may only take four or five solid use cases to discover the commonalities hiding among these quirky early customer situations.

Borrowing lightly from Sigmund's couch therapy, I like to meet with one thoughtful prospect at a time in a relaxed setting, get her/him talking, then try to listen for a solid hour. Having a white board and a second person to take notes allows some steering toward needs and details:

- What is their core business: making hats, transplanting kidneys or trading stocks?
- Where is the pain? Is the buyer awake at night fretting about defect rates, flagging innovation or lost shipments? We need to hear **the customer's own words** here, not our hoped-for answers. ("*We're always out of stock on the hottest-selling dress, but overstocked on last week's favorite...*")
- What constitutes success? Some customers are obsessed with cost savings, others want to reduce downtime or get home in time for dinner. ("*Prove that you can reduce commodity trading time by two seconds, and I'll buy twenty of your servers.*")
- How the problem is being solved today -- since our product isn't yet available? Hint: we'll have to fit into the same architecture as the thing we replace.
- How much does today's solution cost? True operational savings is always the best sales pitch.

- What requirements did the customer specifically call out? Which requirements are so obvious as to be unspoken?
- Are we a fit? Should we pursue this opportunity or run like the wind?

Afterwards, the rest of the team should get a short write-up that lets everyone immerse themselves in the details of a real-world situation, which is much more reliable than Freud's dream interpretations.

SOUND BYTE

Nailing down a few hard-nosed customer use cases is the fastest way to move from "I hope" to "Several customers have told us." Nothing focuses a development team faster than a product manager who can really describe what customers want. Feel free to pass it off as mind reading.

Sharks, Pilot Fish
and the Product Food Chain

W hen you're launching a new venture, one of your earliest considerations is how your innovation might fit into the existing technical environment: should it replace some dominant species or improve the overall market climate? In ecological terms, is your new company going to produce fish food or fight the largest carnivores for survival? And how should that decision shape the company you create?

The IT economy is an ocean crowded with products of every size and description. Engineers and marketers have tried to fill every niche with technical products, many of which have failed to thrive. If you're working on plans for a new technology, it's important to consider where you fit in the product food chain – what's your strategy to survive and thrive?

Just as it takes a vibrant, varied community of plants and herbivores for the few biggest species to survive, there may be many more opportunities for niche successes than for bare-toothed market dominance. So, before whipping up some PowerPoints for VCs that show a $1B market for a $70M investment, consider a few broad options:

1. **Be a shark:** Try to bite off a big chunk of a major market. You'll need to cannibalize major portions of an incumbent shark's product line to succeed, while avoiding sharp teeth.

2. **Be a pilot fish:** Find a profitable niche that complements and improves the solution offered by the big fish. Fill some narrow customer-perceived weaknesses in the incumbent's existing solution without threatening its survival.

3. **Make fish food:** Create specialty, high-value components that the big fish can't or won't make for themselves – but can OEM from you and improve their offerings.

Pondering each model may help clarify your business plan.

HOW ABOUT AN EXAMPLE?

Imagine your housemate is a database wizard and Stanford PhD. She has a prototype that runs complicated reports and queries 180 times faster than Oracle's existing database. You've been asked for a product vision and introductions to a few venture capital folks. This might be a whale of an idea – transforming the $5B database market – or a goldfish-sized footnote.

Building a new product is like creating a new species: you need to plan a survival strategy, then equip your company with the right tools and structure (ecology). The company you build mirrors your expected place in the food chain -- how you plan to build, sell and support this new creature. Each approach has unique risks and opportunities, and it is very difficult to change strategies later. Which of these seems like the best fit for your innovation?

BEING A SHARK: THE FULL SYSTEM SELL

Perhaps your solution is radically different, nothing like today's databases. Maybe data is converted into laser beams, mixed via fiber optics to generate intense color patterns, and etched into reusable light-sensitive silicon pyramids. This is such a leap forward that current database technologies will become extinct. Co-existence isn't possible.

This dramatic evolution calls for a full system sale: replacing the dominant carnivore. Customers will need to gut their Oracle (or DB2 or SQL Server) databases, abandon their environment, swim in a new direction. You will have to convince them of huge advantages, since customers have invested heavily in their current solution.

To compete with the big fish, you'll need a direct, enterprise-class sales team plus glossy marketing materials, big reference customers and endorsements from industry analysts. Customers will have long selling cycles, high expectations, and will need to see your product perform against the competition. Market visibility is a challenge, with so many companies stirring up the sea floor.

The incumbents will counter-attack using their size and market power: highlighting the risk in an unproven technology; identifying checklist items you are missing; rallying reference accounts and executive contacts; raising regulatory barriers; offering polished technical training; serving up more complete platforms and Internationalized versions. They have large, well-trained competitive teams circling to find your weaknesses. Still, there's good eating if you can survive and thrive.

Even though VCs like to fund these major carnivore concepts, few new species survive in the wild. They starve before they can mature. It's taken decades to supplant mainframe dinosaurs, years for wireless to chase away dial-up, and we're still waiting for self-healing networks.

PILOT FISH: EXTENDING THE ECOSYSTEM

If you help the big fish improve their solutions, you don't need to fight them. You can swim alongside the sharks and keep their customers happy. This strategy is sometimes called "partnering" or "joining the ecosystem." In our database example, imagine that you can sell Oracle customers a special tool that makes their existing reports run 100 times faster. Here, our goal isn't to replace Oracle, but to extract money from their customers by filling a product-sized niche. Lower risk, smaller rewards.

By definition, your customers are already buying from the sharks. Most of your marketing and selling activities, then, will revolve around this ecosystem. You will be joining database partner programs, buying lists of Oracle and DB2 customers, and speaking at user groups. Most importantly, you will need to make friends with Oracle's own sales teams and prove to them that you make their customers happier without threatening their commissions. You're one of the pilot fish swimming with the sharks.

The classic challenge with this strategy is to make your extension just valuable enough. If very few customers need your whiz-bang report accelerator, you'll starve for revenue. On the other hand, if every Oracle customer demands it, your big fish will announce it as a future enhancement or be forced to ship a decent alternative. There is always pressure for sharks to add "me too" features once the market has been proven.

MAKING FISH FOOD: OEM FEATURES

One last strategy is to sell directly to the sharks: make a specialty food they need to stay competitive. This is truly a niche approach: create some compelling intellectual property ahead of the market, and have the major players deliver it to customers for you. Think of this as technical vitamins, strengthening and fortifying the big fish. You will need some very rare expertise and a few key customers who demand that the sharks include your special improvement.

Returning to our database example, perhaps no one at Oracle is smart enough – or focused enough – to come up with your database report accelerator. If you can rally some of their major accounts to complain loudly, you may create a need for an internal product team to license your smarts. Every shark's Engineering team is overcommitted, understaffed, and short on focus.

This is an all-or-nothing approach, however. There may be only 2 or 3 big fish in your market, and getting even one to bite will be difficult. Engineering teams are notorious for rejecting outside solutions ("not invented here"). If customers are truly requesting what you sell, the sharks will have some alternate approach to the problem on their development roadmap – to be completed in the next few years – and can plausibly delay you long enough for your venture to starve.

Organizationally, an OEM company should have only a few senior sales folks, and most of its staff in Engineering. You must keep your bit of technology ahead of the market to avoid being marginalized. Do this well, and your whole company may get snapped up.

SOUND BYTE

Big fish need a lot of food and room to swim. Major new competitors invite existing predators to bite back. When planning a new company, you need to decide how big a fish you want to be, and the best organization to support it. Don't swim with sharks just for the halibut.

Insider Thinking

Product managers and other product champions spend a lot of their time driving internal processes and decisions – the daily incremental struggle for progress on pricing, packaging, release schedules, upgrade policies and other bits of the production puzzle. This relentless motivation is indispensable, the tech equivalent of keeping the trains running on time. PMs **should also** be spending time with customers, refreshing their sense of needs and marketplaces.

It's easy to get stuck at headquarters, chairing meetings and shepherding action items. Being important is habit-forming. In fact, the more you drive as product champion, the easier it is to be shackled with additional internal responsibilities. Too long without a road trip, though, and you can lose that visceral sense of customer reactions. I call this problem "insider thinking:" losing touch with external success by over-focusing on the details of delivery processes.

I'm recently back from a road trip to customers and industry press – the best way to combat insider thinking. The trip called to mind some oft-seen examples (with products and markets changed to protect the guilty).

PACKAGING BY ORGANIZATION

You're bringing out a new database product that sometimes needs a separately delivered device driver. *Why is it separate?* Internally, you have a very rational explanation about... divisional revenue recognition and how the Networking Drivers group needs to track shipments to justify its effort. Or uncoordinated release schedules. Or the terms of a restrictive license agreement. Or having a common set of part numbers across all divisions. Or because changing a software bill-of-materials takes months of political infighting.

Within days, Customer Support is getting calls from customers who can't install your latest release. Most callers have ignored a README and several product bulletins explaining that updated network drivers are required, and must be ordered separately. Even worse, the sales force keeps submitting new orders without the specially discounted driver package ("DP8410-db-linux") that they've been briefed on.

Insider thinking has you steamed: "What more can I do to educate customers about the need for supplemental driver packages? RTFM!" Outsiders have a simpler view, though: "**How could you ship me something that doesn't work**?" Your company's organizational problems are of no interest to paying customers, so should never be part of your packaging strategy.

In a real-world parallel, parents will be whispering obscenities this December as they try to assemble holiday gifts for their children. Including a 20-cent Allen wrench with the bicycle kit might be helpful. Or a sticker that reads "nearly-impossible-to-find-batteries not included."

COST-BASED PRICING

Prospects will compare your prices to the competition, and ask why yours is higher. (Somehow, it always is.) Good answers are about customer value: extended support, saved time, more features, ROI, customer endorsements, or product integration.

Your insider thinking is showing, though, if your prices are justified by inputs. Customers rarely care if you have more expensive engineers on the team, or headquarters is demanding profitability, or you signed an unfavorable license agreement with Microsoft. Don't mention that you're using outdated memory boards, or that Purchasing forgot to buy in bulk.

[*For instance, Apple iPods are priced by song capacity, not at 35% above cost-of-goods. Likewise, we choose heart surgeons based on reputation and referral, not on least cost per valve replacement or their Porsche payments.*]

Decide internally if you can compete, behind closed doors. Chain an MBA or two to spreadsheets until you understand breakeven and ROI for each new project before launching the latest teen-targeted PDA or Wi-Fi clearinghouse. Once the decision is made, though, start pitching customer value – and hide the insider thinking.

TALKING TO YOURSELF

At a trade show, random attendees ask what your company does. Pulling out your cue card, you recite something about the "dominant OEM vendor of mid-market, cross-platform storage optimization algorithms." After a few dumbfounded looks, you try again with "our software helps squeeze more data onto disk drives."

What happened? You've dragged out a complex internal positioning statement, painfully built by a marketing-engineering committee. Motivated by the best insider thinking, PM spent months drawing competitive matrices to show Gartner Group how your start-up is slightly better positioned than your VC-backed arch-enemies

Unfortunately, most customers have never heard of you **or your competitors**. They don't care if you focus on the mid-market or that your archrival only runs on Windows. There's not a single meaningful word in this positioning mumbo. Spending some time with prospects (alongside the sales team) reduces your jargon level and refreshes your customer vocabulary.

INSIDE THE BELTWAY

National politics is an extreme case of insider thinking: sometimes news and decisions from Washington DC are inexplicable to folks half a continent away. The internal complications of political decision-making and fundraising can result in odd or contradictory outcomes. We often refer to career politicians and lobbyists as "inside the Beltway" that circles Washington and its near suburbs, and their art-of-the-possible solutions as "inside the Beltway thinking." Here's to being an Outsider with only the market to answer to.

FAKE COMPARISONS

We've all reverse-engineered competitive matrices to look good. These are the familiar checklists of features and benefits that prove we outshine the other guys. (They have a similar matrix that outscores us.) Often, we reach too far.

These fake comparisons don't award any check marks to the competition, and include obviously silly advantages. ("Day and night operation" for flashlights comes to mind.) Choked with insider thinking, they insult the customer. Smart customers will have several versions and judge you on your helpfulness. *[Even if you forget, competitors will mention that your hardware failed FCC radio testing or is suspected of causing blindness.]*

Online ROI calculators suffer a similar fate. We've trained customers to view these very skeptically, especially when the expected savings is impossible to measure. You may be more helpful to prospects by providing the elements and assumptions needed for a custom cost justification – rather than jumping to unexplainably great results.

Hoping for naïve customers is insider thinking. Providing customers with relevant, meaningful product comparisons helps them through the selling cycle. Coincidentally, this is also good marketing.

SOUND BYTE

Stuck at headquarters, it's easy to forget customer realities and needs. Great PMs know that internal goals and criteria are only one part of a successful product. Frequent escapes to talk with live customers are essential to remind us of what's important.

The Strategic Secret Shopper

'**ve** often played the "secret shopper," hired to approach key competitors **as a customer** or as a consultant to a prospective customer. The goal is to find out in detail what the Other Guys are really saying about themselves -- and about you -- plus specifics on their products, pricing, positioning, channels and delivery dates.

It's very difficult for insiders to do this because [1] return phone calls to their office voicemail give away the game immediately, [2] competitive analysis needs consistency and concentration during several weeks of sporadic discussions, and [3] internal product managers/product marketers already **believe** they know the answers.

This last item is key: opinions and product impressions are very sticky, and hard to adjust. If you're a product champion who has been following the Other Guys for a few quarters (or years), your beliefs often get in the way of hearing new messages and spotting trends. In addition, your role is to train your Sales and Channels on the Other Guys' weaknesses – not to present a balanced view of strengths and shortcomings. Instinctively, you want to contradict instead of listen.

In strong contrast, customers and prospects listen to sales pitches with a fresh ear. They catch the strategic themes and general tone, with fewer biases. Most have not studied your offering, so they don't raise the sticky detailed questions that you would. The sales process is partly educational: buyers actually listen to what's being said.

Therefore, getting an **outsider** to shop the competition cuts through the emotional clutter, and sometimes helps identify what's new in the selling cycle. Like real customers, secret shoppers can listen to the highlights of the Other Guys' pitch before getting swamped in low-level details.

ILLEGAL? UNETHICAL?

Being a secret shopping is deceptive. In fact, it requires lying. What are the boundaries of good behavior and good taste? Recognizing that companies **will** try to understand the competition, I'd suggest a few ground rules:

- Respect the rep's time. Get what you need, and get off the phone. Remember that you're taking sales time away from real customers, and "your" rep has a quota to reach. Assume that the Other Guys are reciprocally wasting a little of your reps' time.

- Don't sign an NDA. The game is over once legal documents come out. I wouldn't hire someone who flouts the Other Guys' NDA, since he may handle my internal information accordingly. The Valley is very small, and reputations matter.

- Find additional ways to listen. These include win/loss interviews, quizzing industry analysts, and periodically debriefing the sales team. Attend their seminars. They combine into a well-rounded picture of the competition.

Anything you'd hesitate to tell your client (or your mother) is probably out of bounds, like inviting the Other Guy's employees to job interviews.

ISN'T ALL OF THIS INFORMATION PUBLIC?

In some industries, pricing and products are well known. Airlines, for instance, must publish all of their fares and schedules – and are constantly scanning each other's offerings. Consumer products giants send their junior brand managers out for store checks (walking the supermarket aisles in Des Moines and Savannah) to record local detergent prices and shelf placement. Electronics companies buy competing gear and disassemble it.

Tech start-ups don't always publish their prices or their customer presentations, however. The smart ones are constantly tuning their messages (and products) as the market evolves. High-level positioning shifts when early customers raise new issues - or discover new applications.

OK. Time for me to put on my Secret Shopper hat and cloak, and map out a research project. Imagine that HermitCrab Corp has come out of its shell and hired me to get details on its fierce competitor, PufferFish Technologies. HermitCrab needs sales messages, features, pricing and any notable product shortcomings.

INVENTING A STRATEGIC PROSPECT

The first step in strategic shopping is to **create the customer that I'll pretend to represent**. This isn't HermitCrab, but a likely prospect for both HermitCrab and PufferFish. To keep organized, let's call our imagined customer Zephyr.

Zephyr needs to be a battleground customer, stuck solidly between HermitCrab's offering and PufferFish's. HermitCrab wants to know how to win the toss-up deals, and I need a rationale for asking the kinds of questions that toss-up prospects should ask.

Generally, I'd craft a dossier on Zephyr: revenue, staff size, core market, problem description, quotes from imagined end users, geography, technical buying criteria, internal politics, and purchase timeline. The goal is to formulate a prospect that smells like HermitCrab's last ten competitive accounts. When reviewing this with the HermitCrab sales force, they should recognize every aspect. (When they insist this is a **real** company, and demand contact info, I've done a good job.)

Why bother? These are the details that good salespeople ask for, so I'll need to be prepared. A real customer would know every facet of his situation.

Once I know my mythical client intimately, I'm ready to call PufferFish. Some notes to myself:

- Make the first call on Friday afternoon. Reps who have made quota are already gone, and the hungriest newbies are stuck by the phone.

- Getting good information takes three or four calls. The first call sets up a discussion, instead of concluding one. Don't try to learn everything in ten minutes.

- Explain the situation briefly (*"My client is looking for a product that..."*) and then listen. Carefully. Take lots of notes. Offer up a few details from the dossier only as needed. Don't use the Zephyr name, since good sales folks will quickly discover that my client is a figment.

- Listen for strategic selling themes. Customers may forget product details, but remember the overall story. How does this theme position PufferFish, and how does it undermine Hermit-Crab?

- Save (or screen-capture) the presentation and sales materials. HermitCrab will want to see exactly what prospects see.

- Ask about HermitCrab in passing. Does the PufferFish rep know HermitCrab's products? Anything to consider when evaluating both products? Knock-offs?

- Have a short list of specific questions that need answers. These are items that HermitCrab is worried about. When the list is complete, get off the phone.

Finally, I'd write up impressions of the process: what would a real prospect think? Feel? What land mines has PufferFish planted for HermitCrab? The information needs to be objective, specific, and unemotional. Arguments about whether PufferFish honestly positions HermitCrab are irrelevant.

SOUND BYTE

Every sales force needs to know what their prospects may hear from the competition. One good source is outside "shoppers" who are more open-minded (and less frenzied) than internal product teams. Combining this with other field data is a good way to spot shifts and trends in the marketplace.

Avoiding a Ticking B-O-M

JULY 2002

I n our enthusiasm to get started on software projects, we often jump right into the coding and UI design that make software fun. I've done it. A few weeks before final shipment, though, someone identifies a missing item that costs the team some sleepless nights – or a month's schedule slip. Perhaps it sounds like this...

"We're going to beta on Tuesday and just realized that we need a license agreement for the software installer. Does anyone know who our lawyers are?"

Let's talk about how a "Whole Product Bill of Materials" can save both you and your customers a lot of grief.

The hardware world has always known about Bills of Materials, also called B-O-Ms (pronounced "bombs"). GM and Honda have armies of BOM specialists who can recite the parts inventory for a transmission plus every supplier's production lead time.

Among free-spirited software start-ups, there's usually a good list of the key software modules that have to be written. *(Larry works on the installer, Sarah has database access, Vijay owns the user interface...)* However, many of the essential parts of a software product are not software. Seemingly little things like **toll-free support numbers** and **upgrade paths** are often neglected, but are critical to customer success. A complete Marketing Requirements Document should have a Bill of Materials but usually doesn't.

BEST PRACTICES

I've had a lot of success holding a few brainstorming meetings very early in the product planning process, inviting clear thinkers from Support and Operations as well as Marketing and Engineering. Starting with a clean white board, we talk through the mechanics of **exactly** how a user will get and install our great new software product, then ask for help and handle upgrades. At every step, we list the things that must exist for the customer to succeed on the whole product bill of materials (BOM).

A cross-functional team is key to making this work, including some naive participants as well as very experienced folks. The entire group then walks through each step for the customer, trying to imagine what could go wrong. Here's the very first step, and what we might discover:

"THE USER DOWNLOADS A TRIAL VERSION FROM OUR WEBSITE AND RUNS THE INSTALLER..."

- Marketing: "Before getting to the download, the user should have to fill out a web form with some contact info."

- Support: "Trial versions should have 30 day licenses and time-outs, so that we don't support trial users forever."

- Naive user: "If the installer doesn't work, who do I call (since the help files were not unpacked by the installer)?"

- Operations: "The FTP server might be down. We need a way to monitor the download server, especially if it is hosted somewhere else."

SOUND BYTE

One way to disaster-proof your product cycle is with a whole product Bill of Materials effort to kickstart your thinking. In combination with a solid MRD, this gives you a good start. Don't let your customers teach you what's missing from your product.

Technical Advantage and Competitive Strategy

Products with true technical advantage are rare - and fleeting. Most offerings are lightly differentiated, or not at all. When I hear product folks touting their unbeatable technical superiority, I stop to listen for the footsteps of competitors.

PURE TECHNICAL ADVANTAGE

A handful of products are so clearly advanced that their features define their early market position: *60 miles per gallon in the city. Non-invasive brain survey with radiation beams. Gigabit wireless data transfer. First manned commercial space vehicle.* **Velcro.** Product managers fantasize about having products/services so clearly differentiated, and so far ahead of the market, that they seem to sell themselves.

Early adopters need some specific help understanding and buying your breakthrough product (or service). Typically, they look to you to:

- Explain the value of your technology clearly and persuasively, in terms of benefits and simple use cases
- Provide financial justification so technical users can sell their financial managers on spending money.

Of course, it's never that easy – and a complacent, narrow view of customer alternatives can make you a target. For instance... in the early '90's Sybase had the first database with "stored procedures." These event triggers let Wall Street create program trading: computers that could make real-time decisions about buying and selling stocks. Sybase grabbed a lucrative spot in the back offices of investment banks, but (within a few years) found itself out-positioned, out-sold and out-blustered by Oracle and other database players. Each vendor claimed similar capabilities, and had persuasive ways of shifting the discussion.

THE NATURE OF THE THREAT

If you actually have a technical lead on your market, it pays to think through how emerging competitors will try to unseat you. The US Army calls this "red teaming." Let's consider a new company that's late to the market but has similar technical solutions to our enterprise-focused problem. Assume they have some smart product marketers (trained to sell today's less-than-perfect current offering) as well as product managers (wrestling to make next quarter's release better).

Your "red team" is likely to pick a few of these tactics:

- **Find an unserved segment.** Your whiz-bang database might lack proper audit controls for banks, or wide enough fields for DNA sequencing scientists. Late-arrivers can spot customer groups that you missed entirely.

- **Bundle and package.** Microsoft, Oracle and Cisco often toss decent-but-colorless products into existing product suites with very little incremental cost. This helps starve single-product competitors.

- **Partner with the big boys.** If you can get Yahoo (or IBM or Pfizer) to mention, endorse or co-market your product, it impresses customers. Even if the big boys never come through with a single sale of their own.

- **Marketecture.** Savvy product marketers can always describe their solution as a better fit with standards, upcoming technologies, industry leaders and the customer's own roadmap. Somehow, you are positioned as narrow and inflexible: a one-product company who arrived too early to see the important trends.

- **New pricing metric.** Perhaps some customer segments prefer to pay per month (or per meal, per gigabyte, per job applicant, per virus detected) instead of your enterprise-wide annual license. Consider multiple pricing models.

- **Sell high to non-techies.** Customers use cross-functional teams to evaluate major purchases. Competitors may focus on the CFO, the compliance officer, or dangle a related sales opportunity in front of the customer's VP of Sales. Part of selling is identifying the "choosers" as well as the "users."

There's no magic here: other product folks will apply these tried-and-true strategies to take away your technical advantage.

SO WHAT SHOULD WE DO?

Start by realizing that technical selling is not a purely rational process. You need to **understand your target market deeply**, plan your next several competitive moves, and then arm your sales force with both rational and emotional tools to close the deal. Not only feature comparisons, but also usage scenarios with clear benefits, and perceptive stories that carefully position your company. Plus solid ROI justification for the finance folks.

Avoid technology-driven optimism. Competitors may already be offering substitutes to your (apparently) superior solution. Even those players with technically inferior products are working to distract customers and re-arrange perceptions. We often see "better" products lose to mediocre – but well-marketed – alternatives.

 SOUND BYTE

It's easy to believe your own hype about technically superior products, especially if it's true. Regardless, you still need to listen for the footsteps behind you – and plan competitively.

Mo' Beta

A t some time in every product cycle, the executive team wants to help product management "improve" its customer beta process. This is generally because the last beta took too long, didn't get enough useful customer feedback, or failed to prime the revenue pump for a post-GA sales blitz. Notice that these three goals are mutually exclusive...

One way out of the beta dilemma is to recognize the different audiences and objectives for a beta cycle, then structure different programs for each. Here, I've sorted beta prospects into three camps: the **Loyal Opposition**, the **Overcommitted**, and the **Reluctant Volunteers**.

THE LOYAL OPPOSITION

These are the most fanatical technologists among your current customer base. If you're big enough to have a user group, the Loyal Opposition crowds into late afternoon roadmap sessions to trade configuration tips and lobby for missing features. They love your product almost as much as they love pointing out minor errors.

If you don't already, you should pamper the Loyal Opposition. During beta testing, they will shred your pre-release software, grammar-check your documentation, and invent bizarre uses for your new features. (These are all good things!) They **don't generate any short-term incremental revenue**, though, because they are already paying customers.

Plan as many early code drops as you can to the Loyal Opposition: this supplements your internal QA effort with unconventional thinking. Consider a limited edition t-shirt for those who find bugs, and keep your sales team away from these eccentric gems. Drop compliments about them in obscure USENET locations.

THE OVERCOMMITTED

These customers and prospects are easy to recognize: they call your sales team frequently for assurance that your release is still on schedule. In the extreme, they have built their own product or service delivery schedule around your GA release dates – and have no slack. When your GA delivery date inevitably slips, they are in deep water.

Including the Overcommitted in your beta program is required, not optional. It gives your sales team a face-saving way to gloss over promises, and gives customers a hope of hiding their optimism. You may grumble and refuse initially, but expect to be overruled by the VP Sales.

Overcommitted beta customers are high risk, though. They will expect production-ready products that are fully tested, since your sales team has given them this impression. Some will put your "early GA release" directly into production. If your testing cycle has been shortened to recover lost engineering time, you may have a disaster on your hands. Try to assign a support engineer or smart field SE to each account, and be prepared to demand some very quick fixes from Engineering.

RELUCTANT VOLUNTEERS

Let's be realistic: most beta customers never install your product. Your handcrafted CD and installation manual will probably be shelved next to 80 other untouched beta products.

Reluctant Volunteers come from a pair of mistaken impressions: sales teams think that beta installations will help close deals faster, and CIOs think their network managers (or sys admins, or database experts, or help desk teams, or software architects) have idle time to play with new stuff. Your sales rep "calls high" and convinces the customer's CIO to be a beta site. When this trickles down the org chart, no one offers to give up another weekend to debug your code. *(If you look up "passive aggressive" in the dictionary, you'll see a picture of a Reluctant Volunteer.)*

You'll spend most of your beta program chasing Reluctant Volunteers. Consider asking each for a test plan as a rapid way to sort the interested few from the uninvolved many.

Recapping:

Group	Result	Revenue	Risk
Loyal Opposition	Real feedback if given a long beta cycle	None	None
Overcommitted	May save face for sales rep and customer	Some	High
Reluctant Volunteers	None	None	Wasted effort

SOUND BYTE

In theory, we all love beta testing. In practice, loyal customers are joined by a few panicked prospects in a rush to general release. This generates scant feedback and minimal revenue. If you want useful results, plan a long beta phase for friendly customers followed by a short, post-QA cycle for urgent situations.

What Should Things Cost?

Most discussions about pricing are really about specific prices. Does milk cost $2 or $3 per gallon? Can I fly to Boston for less than $500? Can I afford to spent $20,000 to install solar on the roof of my house?

For me, the more interesting discussion happens long before we assign a specific price to a product (or service). Can we shape our customers' behavior and their perception of us by changing the **basis of pricing**? Using the above examples, organic rBST-free milk might be worth $5 per gallon to the right consumers. Airlines mark up non-stops and discount red-eye flights. Berkeley is experimenting with tax credits and financing (such as long-term loans that mimic mortgages) to encourage installation of residential photovoltaic systems.

Similarly, what if we gave software developers bonuses that decreased with each legitimately reported bug? Or an upstart cell phone company offered to refund subscription fees if they dropped calls? I'm ready to pay extra to my appliance repairman for narrowing his arrival time from "some time Tuesday morning" to "between 9AM and 10AM." Or to any store with shoes that fit my narrow feet.

Smart pricing strategists look for ways to shift the basis of competition, and to offer unique options by segments. This requires a keen sense of what's important to customers, how they react to pricing, and what happens inside the head of a sales rep. I hope you'll generate some unique models of your own.

"Goldilocks" Packaging

Established companies in established markets generally have some standard ways to package and price their new offerings. Product extensions are benchmarked against the existing product line or the other guy's features and prices. This leaves product managers focusing on "faster, cheaper, better, more."

In a brand-new market, though, there are fewer guideposts. Close competitors may not exist. Even before final products are ready, you need to define initial packaging and pricing for your fledgling sales force and prospects. Otherwise, the sales team will invent it haphazardly, one visit at a time. Here's a starter approach that I've called "Goldilocks" packaging.

Borrowing lightly from the fairy tale, we want to construct three pricing packages with increasing feature sets. We hope that prospects will think of them as "too small, too big, and j-u-s-t right!" Why three? Huge consumer products companies that measure buying behavior tell us that we like to have three options (whether for hamburger meals or SUV models or external hard drives). When faced with more than three choices, we get confused and may postpone a purchase. With fewer, we don't notice that each package **has** any features.

Even more important, we want to sell on **features** as well as size. Our customers don't know how much they need (in obscure product metrics like "virus scans per hour" or "GB of trading data"), so we want to offer functional reasons to trade up. The goal of "Goldilocks" packaging is to create three distinct versions that appeal to different buying audiences. Of course, it's critical to know which of your features are the "must have" items at each level, so that your hungry sales force will have a way to upsell customers into bigger packages.

HOW ABOUT AN EXAMPLE?

Imagine that you've founded a start-up targeting the latest generation gap[4] in office communications: Instant Messaging (IM) and its conversational shortcuts. Corporations are being forced to keep audit logs of IM chat -- and forty-something IT directors are struggling to understand their twenty-somethings' crazy IM abbreviations. Here's a market ripe for innovation.

This is a completely new niche, so prospects can't size their need. ("How do I know how many MB/sec these crazy Instant Message kids use?") So, we'd prefer to scale our packages by features as well as capacity. Assuming that our brilliant developers

---

4. This is a very dated example now that IM is on every desktop. Feel free to substitute the latest social networking widget or hot new thing, but the lesson doesn't change.

can work miracles overnight, here are a few cool reasons for upsell:

Package	Features	Price
Entry	<ul><li>Logs 2 simultaneous IM conversations</li><li>10 MB storage</li><li>Browser-based archive search (find all "*lol cid gmta*")</li></ul>	$2,000 per appliance
Department	<ul><li>Logs up to 20 simultaneous IM conversations</li><li>100 MB storage</li><li>Can display traditional English equivalent ("*k otp g2g*" also shown as "**OK, on the phone, got to go.**")</li></ul>	$6,000 per appliance
Enterprise	<ul><li>Logs up to 200 simultaneous IM conversations</li><li>20 GB optical storage</li><li>Fault-tolerant, dual-processor</li><li>High-efficiency cache for emoticons</li><li>Email-to-IM bridging. Sets up a translated conversation between Instant Messaging and email users. (Boss sends "strategic downsizing" email and code geek receives a "chek out MnsterBord" instant message)</li></ul>	$40,000 per cluster

Notice that the new features signal their intended audiences. A department manager who is IM-clueless will still need the mid-sized package to learn that "*lol cid gmta*" means "**laughing-out-loud: consider it done. Great minds think alike**." Email traditionalists will buy the big version and deny the IM's existence. We've given each buyer some reasons to pick the one that's *j-u-s-t* right. Here's a hint: upselling features is much easier than estimating some customer's peak IM usage.

Likewise, broadly different prices help a customer choose quickly. Cash-strapped tire kickers buy low; corporate committees with lists of disaster recovery requirements buy high. We've also saved Sales the embarrassment of inventing products on the fly.

 SOUND BYTE

Packaging and pricing help our customers buy what we make. In particular, software features are a great way to differentiate your Baby Bear, Mama Bear and Papa Bear packages. That keeps your anxious sales team from selling strictly on price before you've established the natural product boundaries of your new market.

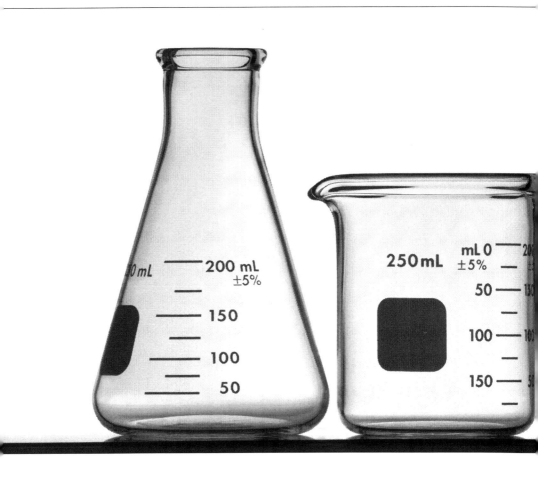

What's Your Pricing Metric?

APRIL 2003

'm often involved in pricing discussions, which are typically introduced as "what's the right price for my product?" Much more important is the strategy that should precede this question, namely "what is the right **pricing unit** for my product and my market?"

An example: Imagine that we've seen the success of various network appliances – firewalls, email servers, VPNs – and want to capture the next appliance market. Our technical team has built a gadget that corrects grammar in emails and memos as they are sent out, making all of our customers sound well educated. How will we price it? More specifically, what's the right **pricing metric**?

There are lots of alternatives… we could sell an appliance based on its raw throughput (5M bits/sec of email, or 50M bits/sec). We could also imagine setting prices by the document, per word, per user, or as a monthly lease. In a twist on "paying for performance," we might give away the service and charge only for the corrections that are made – careful, well-schooled users pay nearly nothing.

WHICH SHOULD I PICK?

A priori, none of these is necessarily better than another. We have to match them against our target customers. What do our customers need, and how will they want to buy?

- Most corporate software buyers are used to per-user pricing for desktop applications like virus protection and MS Office. Our easiest selling strategy for these mainstream businesses could be a **per-seat price**, upgrading to whatever size appliance is needed to handle the load. Hot swap units seem like an obvious upsell to this audience.

- Large insurance companies will need huge stacks of memos processed, so are likely to buy appliances outright – and will need a **throughout pricing** model in documents-per-hour. They will also want to lock down the style options ("long-winded, complex, obscure") for a consistent tone.

- An online proofreading service for university students probably wants a **transaction model**: charging students for each essay turned from straw into gold. If we want to sell into this ASP market, a per-word or per-page charge would match their revenue with our pricing. Providing word counts and document tracking would also make their billing processes easier.

- ISPs and mail hosting providers could offer a "grammar check" option for a few additional dollars per month per subscriber. Knowing how risk-averse ISPs are, we might offer a **revenue-sharing** model and take half of the ongoing subscription.

- Corporate HR departments might want to buy this for hand-selected management trainees who dress well but are functionally illiterate. The number of people in such a program would be secret, so selling this "per seat" or "per user" won't work. Maybe a **monthly lease** could easily be hidden in an "education for excellence" budget. An upcharge to turn off logging and IP address capture also comes to mind.

You get the point. Our pricing unit depends on whom we sell to, how our product will be used, and how it will be paid for. Unique customer groups may each have their own natural unit of pricing. Parenthetically, as we think about how our customers will use the new grammar appliance, we see that every target market will also need some unique features.

LET'S DO THEM ALL!

What about offering nine kinds of pricing, each in five sizes, to cover all possible buyers? Ouch! You should expect to see at least three kinds of problems:

1. Most buyers can't handle pricing complexity. If you give them too many choices, they will panic. Some may suffer through your sales process, while others vanish forever. Remember that your sales people are also human: their skill is selling, not navigating bizarre spreadsheets.

2. Some buyers are very clever. Presented with many pricing plans, they can figure out which will save them the most. Academics call this "adverse selection" but you can call it "lost revenue." Smart corporate purchasers love to work each of your price plans until they find the one that's nearly free.

3. Targeted discounting doesn't stay targeted. I've seen companies introduce education-only pricing (or "special one-time VAR discounts" or cheaper consumer-labeled versions) while keeping corporate pricing high. Your sales channel won't ask

buyers for their student IDs, and the market will quickly figure out how to qualify for your limited offer.

In short, pricing units are one part of fitting a product into a target segment. Just as with features and support options, a pricing model must be imagined in a specific customer context. Thoughtful pricing isn't generic, but market-specific. Innovative pricing models can open up new segments if the accepted approach creates barriers to buying.

 ## SOUND BYTE

Picking the units for your price plan is strategic, and depends heavily on your target customer. It's also part of your feature-function mix, since different segments will need unique features from your product.

Risk-Sharing and Customer-Perceived Value

Whenever customers buy your product or service, there's a leap of faith that they will get value from you. An alternative is to offer your solution in return for some of the savings – and to measure this in the customer's own business units. Even if you fall back on traditional pricing, it will help the customer assign real value to what you deliver.

An example: my company creates knowledge bases (KB) that store the collected wisdom and policies of technical support teams. We claim to speed up problem resolution time by 20%, saving our customers lots of money. Typical pricing strategies are to price this "by the seat" or "by the month" or "depending on the size of your knowledge base." None of these reflect why your customer is buying this solution.

Consider turning this around, and taking a portion of the actual value you deliver. "We think we will save you 20% of your support costs, or $600,000 per year based on what you spend today. We will give you our product for **free**, but want 10% of the savings. If we're right, you pay us 1/10th of the cost reductions, or $60,000. Pay us less if it saves you less – and don't pay us at all if there are no savings."

Notice how this turns you into a partner, instead of a vendor:

- **You understand the customer's business.** This proposal addresses your buyer's actual need: to reduce support costs, and in language she uses with her own management. Normally, the customer has to hope that purchases will lead to results.

- **The short-term risk is gone.** It's hard to reject a vendor who is willing to work for nothing. The fear that products will be useless ("dead on arrival") is removed. Collectively, corporate technology buyers have been burned many times.

- **Your business interests are aligned.** You have every incentive to make the customer successful, not just collect an up-front commission. This separates you from the many drop-and-run vendors with poor post-sales training and follow-through.

SOUNDS GREAT, I THINK...?

On the flip side, these arrangements create a different set of risks for both parties. You are now tightly linked, jointly committed to delivering the savings that you promised. Dangers and concerns:

- **You didn't get paid yet.** If your company needs hard cash for payroll and electricity, this isn't it. CFOs and auditors will be unhappy with risk-sharing or revenue-sharing deals, and will insist on deferring sales commissions until the actual money arrives. Revenue may trickle in over several quarters or years.

- **Customer implementations matter.** Even the best products are worthless when not implemented, and some customers will never get things right. You now have to motivate and instigate a good outcome, even if it takes more resources than you planned.

- **Measurement is hard.** Defining precise and fair metrics for cost savings or incremental revenue is tough. You may be wrestling about what costs are "included" in relevant savings, or how much additional revenue would have come in without your brilliant marketing program.

- **You may ultimately be overpaid.** Customers should do some mental math about upsides, not just downsides. If your new web commerce application brings in $100M in new business instead of $8M, are they still willing to pay you 10%?

In a famously apocryphal story, one big computer company 'gave' a mainframe computer to Sabre early in the development of airline reservation systems. The system was delivered at no charge, but with a cents-per-transaction agreement that would continue paying for the life of the application. Over the years, this was dramatically more than the initial value of the gear.

SO WHO WOULD AGREE TO THIS?

In reality, not many customers will sign up for this kind of split-incentive model. It is hard to define, hard to approve through Accounts Payable, and generally doesn't fit corporate purchasing models. It can still help you close a traditionally priced sale for services or products -- by forcing customers to calculate your value for themselves. We've turned their ROI into your own ROI and shown how much you can contribute.

Imagine that you are a world-famous designer of automotive plants, offering to help a client reconfigure his truck line. You think you can squeeze out 5% more SUVs per day by re-arranging various steps in the assembly process, and have asked for a portion of the incremental profits. Your client's internal musings go like this:

- *"My plant is building 400 trucks per day now, and Jim thinks he can boost this 5%, to 420. Allocated overhead per truck is $1000, so we would save $20,000 per day in plant and equipment by squeezing out 20 more trucks...*

- *"That's $4M per year. I'm a hero if I can deliver even a piece of this...*

- *"Jim wants 8% of the improvement, though, for the first two years. That's $320k per year. No way that I can get my CFO to sign off on this. Besides, if he does even better, we'll owe him even more. I need to negotiate a fixed fee...*

- *"Wonder if he will settle for a one-time $250k engagement? Then we get to bank the rest of the money we would have paid him."*

In fact, he will probably have this precise discussion with his boss before asking to sign you up. If you can help a client think through your value to him, then justifying a small portion of it shouldn't be so difficult for either of you.

NOT A NEW THING

Historically, we've seen incentive pay for commissioned sales people, Hollywood talent agents, and lawyers taking contingency cases. It's emerging in the web search market ("pay per click").

Pushing this to the extreme, there might be lots of pay-for-performance schemes:

- Direct mail agencies getting higher fees for response rates over 1%
- Academic coaches rewarded for their pupils' SAT scores
- Cable TV companies paid for the number of channels watched, rather than delivered
- Home security patrols with rebates for break-ins
- Product managers who want a small portion of eventual revenues for their MRDs and pricing strategies...

Most of these are fraught with difficulties and moral hazards, but considering them may present some novel opportunities.

SOUND BYTE

Offering to share results and risks with your client enables some exciting discussions. Even if you fall back on more traditional pricing, you've demonstrated your appreciation for the customer's own issues.

Sales-Friendly Price Lists

JANUARY 2004

P rice lists are never quite current enough, sufficiently detailed, or cover enough of the awkward special situations that customers raise. So, there's a tendency for HQ product and pricing folks to do a lot of tinkering on the margins with their price lists. We may be forgetting the "consumers" of price lists, though: sales reps who pay our salaries and customers wondering what to buy. Complicated pricing models may be self-defeating.

First, the necessary disclaimer. I'm someone who takes obscure pleasure in tuning prices and packaging for marginal improvement. Finding a clever way to boost profits by another 1% is an intellectual victory. Rejiggering bundles and suites is a way to signal which products are important. Part numbers beg for housekeeping.

I see hidden costs in excessive revisions to price sheets, though. Let's consider two: slow absorption and excessive complexity.

PUBLISHING ISN'T THE END

Sitting in the corporate ivory tower, it's easy to imagine that publishing a new price list is the **completion** of a process. After intense negotiations among the financial / engineering / marketing folks, you've come to some agreement. At 10AM on a Tuesday, you formally post a new version of your price list to the company website and begin to mail it out to key resellers. In reality, the work has just begun.

Throughout your sales channel and customer base, there are now people with outdated price sheets. Not just the most recent one, but 4 or 5 generations of out-of-date product numbers and configurations and prices. Some copies are pinned to cubicle walls, others are laminated in binders or stapled to slow-moving customer proposals. Even though these are legally invalidated by your new version (*"effective immediately, supercedes all previous"*), the world doesn't stop. And you really don't want your sales force to interrupt deals already in progress.

With an aggressive push, you've started the trickle of new price lists replacing old. Unfortunately, sales teams don't share your fanatical devotion to staying current, and don't want to confuse prospects with new stuff. I usually assume 30 to 90 days for word to get out.

WHAT TO DO?

- **Change as few things as possible.** Assume that resellers and customers will be working from last year's list, so identical prices and product numbers will let them place some of their orders correctly.

- **Choose a regular expiration date** for price lists, perhaps twice per year. Even if nothing is new, the old price sheets will be replaced each January 15th and July 15th. Your biggest challenges will be to get sign-off on all changes before the deadline, and to avoid interim updates.

- If publishing schedules won't work, **tie new price lists to major product announcements.** You will be sending out cartons of new materials anyway – data sheets, presentations, train-the-trainer videos, whatever. *"Since WidgetWare v6.0 replaces v4.0 through 5.9, we are adding its new modules and packaging to our revised price list. Previous price sheets are now obsoleted."*

Remember that price list updates are expensive for you and painful for the recipients. Regardless of the number of changes. Tiny improvements and clarifications are rarely worth the trouble.

KEEPING IT SIMPLE

A bigger problem is an overly complicated price list. This may be a reflection of an overly fussy pricing model that has too many dimensions. *("For 50,000 transactions per month or less, the per-seat charge plus the per-server charge apply except when the customer wants a site license ...")* Mere mortals will never get it right, even with 100 pages of examples.

Similarly, complex price lists may be the accumulation of different usage scenarios. If a PM has failed to choose a target customer and application, she may try to define a half-dozen different ways to buy her product, and wrap each in its own pricing model. *("For hosted applications, see page 3. For pay-per-transaction customers, page 4. One-time licenses plus annual maintenance on page 6.")* In the real world, it's very difficult to define the exact boundary between hosted and leased software, forcing every large sale to be reviewed by Talmudic scholars.

Out in the field, where sales teams wrestle to bring in your paycheck, **pricing should never be the focus of a sales call**. You want your reps to spend prospects' precious time on benefits, solution selling, and creative problem-solving. As soon as pricing becomes the focus, the sales team loses their ability to sell value.

SOUNDS LIKE...

Try on these three customer conversations about an accounting package:

Worst:

- Sales rep: "*...it includes general ledger integration, Sarbanes-Oxley reporting, automatic calculation of Federal and state depreciation, and meets all of the requirements you've listed in your strategic overview.*"
- Customer: "*Great. How's it priced?*"
- Sales rep: "*Well, depending on whether you choose the server-based option with concurrent licensing or the per-seat ASP hosting approach, and estimating your usage at 500 to 1000 completed transactions per week plus 200 MB of downloaded reports and partial support upgrades...*"
- Customer, unspoken: "*My head hurts, and I'll have to run every scenario myself to see which is the best deal.*"

Your masterpiece is alienating customers. Dumb prospects will walk away, and smart ones will force your rep to negotiate against himself. Expect to hear about it later.

Weak:

- Customer: "***Great. How's it priced***?"
- Sales rep: "***I have the Nov-25th price sheet, and it was $215 per seat per year plus options, but there may have been some changes since then. When I get back to my desk, I'll check the online version and send over a quote.***"
- Customer, unspoken: "*I wonder if this guy is disorganized, dishonest, or just works for a screwed-up company.*"

You haven't helped your team close the deal.

Best:

- Customer: "***Great. How's it priced?***"
- Sales rep: "***It's roughly $200 to $240 per seat per year, depending on the options.***"
- Customer "***OK. I'd really like to see you demonstrate the interface with our existing warehouse systems...?***"

Your team sold solutions and benefits. Pricing was never the focus and didn't confuse anyone.

SOUND BYTE

Sales teams want to spend time selling benefits and solutions. Customers want to solve problems, perhaps with the stuff you sell. Pricing is best when it is simple and stable enough to blend into the background.

Afterword

And so it goes. We product managers try to impose order on a chaotic work world, cajoling and negotiating and browbeating to get great products and services into the hands of customers. We're an odd bunch: organizationally challenged and socially marginalized. Smarter folks wonder why we are so persistent.

If you're a product manager and have gotten this far, I'm hoping that you laughed and sighed and groaned a bit. Please join the conversation at www.Enthiosys.com or drop me a line at rich@mironov.com.

Acknowledgements

A great many folks helped make this book possible. I'm especially appreciative of Hank Chesbrough and David Strom for their encouragement by example; Andrea Corney for her editorial insights; Luke Hohmann, Scott Gilbert, Jen Smith and the Enthiosys team for getting us to done-done; the Mironov Consulting office management staff (Katrina, Diva and Eloise); Dave and Selma Mironov for covering the start-ups costs; Roy Albert, John Sebes and Barb Coll, Jenny Coupe, Wade Williamson, Dave Taber, Ken Rock, Mike Ehrlich, Bruce Paton, John Einstoss, Val Swisher, Steve Mezak, David Thompson, and the dozens of others who encourage me to keep putting virtual pen to virtual paper.

About the Author

Rich Mironov is a software product strategist and veteran of four high-tech startups. He is currently Chief Marketing Officer (CMO) of Enthiosys, a product strategy consultancy headquartered in Silicon Valley, where he advises technology companies ranging from F100 to pre-funded startups. Rich is considered an expert on software product management and marketing with a focus on business strategy, pricing and market analysis.

Rich started his technology career as a software engineer at Hewlett-Packard, and product managed networking solutions at Tandem Computers. Later, Rich created and ran Sybase's Internet Products Group, whose web.sql product was the first commercial solution for linking Web pages to databases.

After Sybase, he worked at four Silicon Valley companies: Wayfarer Communications (acquired by Vantive in 1998), iPass (which went public in 2003), Slam Dunk Networks (VP of marketing) and AirMagnet (VP of marketing).

In addition to his continuing column on technology product strategy, Rich is a highly sought-after speaker and writer. He is on the faculty of the Executive Development Center at the University of California Berkeley's Haas School of Business.

Rich has an MBA from Stanford University, and a BS degree in physics from Yale University (with a thesis on dinosaur extinction theories). Half geek and half culture vulture, he lives midway between San Francisco and Silicon Valley.

Made in the USA
Charleston, SC
11 June 2010